EXCAVATIONS IN
STAINES
1975–76

The Friends' Burial Ground Site

K. R. Crouch and S. A. Shanks

1984

Joint Publication No. 2
London & Middlesex Archaeological Society
Surrey Archaeological Society

The Societies are grateful to the Department of the Environment for a substantial contribution towards the cost of publishing this report

ISBN 0-903290-26-X (London & Middlesex Archaeological Society)
ISBN 0-9501345-4-6 (Surrey Archaeological Society)

This report has been edited on behalf of the Societies by Joanna Bird, with assistance from Dr D G Bird (Conservation and Archaeology Section, Surrey County Council) and Dr C J Young (Department of the Environment, Ancient Monuments Inspectorate)

Printed by Adlard & Son Ltd, Dorking, Surrey

Microfiche produced by Surrey Microfilm Services, Guildford, Surrey

EXCAVATIONS IN STAINES, 1975–6: THE FRIENDS' BURIAL GROUND SITE

K R CROUCH and S A SHANKS

On microfiche fiche

London & Middlesex Archaeological Society and Surrey Archaeological Society, Joint Publication No 2.

I INTRODUCTION TO THE ARCHAEOLOGY OF STAINES

K R CROUCH and S A SHANKS

History of archaeological investigation

As early as the 17th century, Camden in his *Britannia* (Camden 1695, 366) suggested that Staines had Roman origins, and identified it as *Pontes*. Stukeley (1726, 205) also referred to Staines by its Roman name (for a fuller discussion of the name *Pontes* see Crouch 1976, 72–3; Rivet & Smith 1979, 441) but it was not until the 19th century, when a large number of chance finds of Roman date were recorded, that substance was added to these earlier statements. Sharpe (1913, 74) listed numerous prehistoric and Roman finds from Staines, and included references to a bath-house and tessellated pavement. He revised and added to his catalogue in the 1930s when the discovery of several groups of complete vessels drew attention to the probable site of a Roman cemetery to the east of the town (Sharpe 1932, 115).

The first modern archaeological work in Staines commenced in 1969, during the development of the Barclays Bank site; this work was carried out by Mrs M Rendell for the then London Museum, and later for the London and Middlesex Archaeological Society, with grants from the Ministry of Public Buildings and Works, subsequently the Department of the Environment. This initial project drew attention to the need for further work, and subsequent small-scale excavations confirmed the findings of the Barclays Bank site (fig 1; Crouch 1976).

By 1973 the large quantities of material recovered from excavation necessitated the employment of a permanent Field Officer and two assistants to follow on from Mrs Rendell's work, and to excavate sites prior to the major redevelopment which was due to start in late 1973 and early 1974. The first site excavated was Elmsleigh House in 1974–5 (Crouch 1976), followed by the Friends' Burial Ground (1975–6), National Westminster Bank (1976), Central Area Development (1977), Bridgehead (1978), and Johnson & Clark (1979) sites (fig 1). In 1979 the continuing pace of development and the amount of work undertaken led to the formation of the Staines Archaeological Unit, which was later incorporated into the archaeological unit within the Surrey County Council Planning Department.

Geology and topography

The underlying 'solid' geology of the area is London Clay, with a top surface at approximately +6.09m OD. Upon this base are a succession of gravel and alluvial layers. The earlier layers were glacial in origin (*eg* outwash gravels); later levels resulted from the activities of the River Thames, such as changes of course and depositional effects (the 'drift' geology). The topography of the Staines area is that of the Thames, its valley and tributaries. *C* 3.2km to the west is a ridge of hills, running north–south, which rise sharply from the valley floor at +16.2m OD to *c* +60.97m OD. The Colne and its tributaries border the north and west of the gravel terrace on which the town is built, and with the Thames to the south form natural defensive boundaries.

Utilisation and occupation

From the information so far obtained it has been established that the site of the present town of Staines has been favoured for occupation, probably since the Mesolithic. Recent archaeological work in the surrounding area shows intensive occupation during all prehistoric periods (Neolithic: Robertson-Mackay 1962; Later Bronze Age: Longley 1976; O'Connell & Needham 1977; Iron Age: Canham 1978b). At Staines Mesolithic, Neolithic and Bronze Age occupation was restricted to a series of gravel islands, and an apparently similar situation is seen at Runnymede (pers comm D Longley) and Kingston (pers comm M Hinton). By the Middle

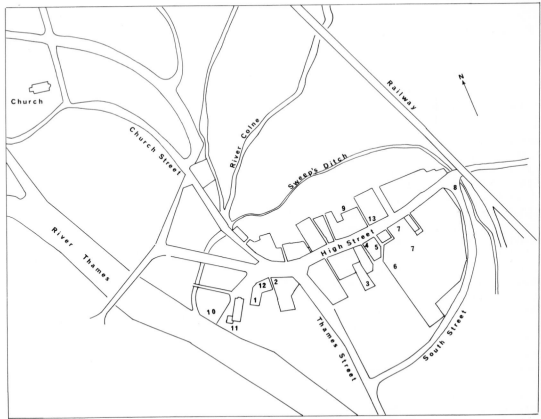

Fig 1. Map of Staines showing excavated sites: 1 Conservative Club; 2 Johnson & Clark; 3 Friends' Burial Ground; 4 National Westminster Bank; 5 Barclays Bank; 6 Elmsleigh House; 7 Central Area Development; 8 Mumford & Lobb; 9 Reeves; 10 Bridgehead; 11 Day Centre; 12 Market Place; 13 Perrings

Bronze Age the intersecting channels had silted up and dried out, permitting occupation over larger areas. During the Later Bronze Age and the Iron Age a gradual rise in the water-table restricted occupation to one central island. By the end of the Iron Age the water table had fallen again, and the land exposed was utilised for the site of a Roman town, perhaps on the position of an already established military base at the river crossing on the route between Camulodunum and Calleva.

Finds from Staines (*cf* Crouch 1976, 73) suggest that the Roman town began as a military base shortly after the Roman conquest, and that this was occupied until after the revolt of Boudica. The position of Staines would make it eminently suitable as a centre for military supplies and communications. Such a military establishment would be soon followed by a civilian settlement, and possible evidence for this was found on the Central Area Development site 1977 (report in preparation), where there were also indications that the civil settlement at least was destroyed by fire *c* AD 60. The date suggests that the destruction was associated with the Boudican revolt and there may have been further military activity at Staines after this date, which lasted only a few years. After the withdrawal of the military, the town continued to expand and, given its situation on the river and a major road, was presumably a place of some importance, perhaps the site of a *mansio* (pers comm J Wacher). This growth in the town is reflected in the increased area occupied.

The earlier, Flavian, buildings were of beam slot construction, replaced during the Trajanic–Hadrianic period by those of a box-framed construction technique (*cf* Drury 1975, 165). Many of these buildings probably served a dual purpose as shop/workshop and residence. Most had walls plastered internally and simply painted with decorative panels in various colours. Excavation suggests that towards the end of the 2nd century many buildings were demolished, much of the town levelled, and the plots left vacant, although some late 2nd and early 3rd century British and continental pottery imports show that trade was still viable. As yet no cause for this decline is known, but a similar sequence of events has been noted at London, Brentford and Southwark (Sheldon & Schaaf 1978, 66–7) and at Chelmsford (Drury 1975, 165).

Some re-establishment apparently took place almost immediately, but during the early 3rd century serious flooding affected the edges of the settlement, depositing up to 1m of silt in some places, and probably causing a contraction in the settlement to the higher area around the present day Market Place and the junction of High Street and Thames Street (fig 1). The period during which the lower-lying areas were rendered uninhabitable is difficult to assess, but evidence from the Friends' Burial Ground suggests between 30 and 50 years. Late in the 3rd or early in the 4th century, there was renewed occupation of the area previously affected by flooding. The nature of settlement here had apparently changed to a series of large individual plots consisting of a house and land on which to grow food, and this suggested increase in horticulture may be one explanation for the 'black earth' deposit which is found throughout the town sealing the earlier levels. Some of the buildings were of timber-framed wattle and daub construction, some of stone. The 4th century was seemingly one of prosperity, and many of the finds indicate that the town was sufficiently prosperous to import goods and materials from other parts of Britain and from the Continent.

In the late 4th and early 5th centuries there seems to have grown up alongside the Romano-British town a small 'Germanic' settlement, indicated by shell-tempered pottery. This occupation was apparently restricted at first to the areas fringing the limits of the late Roman town, but later spread gradually into part of the town proper. In the 5th century grass-tempered pottery first appeared, associated with a small industrial complex (fig 10) sited on the outer fringes of the late Romano-British/'Germanic' settlement. By the middle of the century grass-tempered pottery and stamped wares had entirely replaced the shell-tempered wares, which may indicate continuity of occupation throughout the 5th century. Staines, with its bridge and communication links east and west, may have been one of the areas allegedly protected by *foederati* (Frere 1974, 382) and it is reasonable to suggest that the grass-tempered pottery belongs with their arrival. By the 7th century, grass-tempered pottery alone survived, and these wares lasted through to the Middle Saxon period. For a fuller discussion of the Saxon and Saxo-Norman periods, see Jones (1982).

The late Saxon and subsequent history of Staines has been described in the relevant volume of the VCH (1962). However, an archaeological find of some importance is a recut ditch, apparently of late Saxon date, which may be connected with the Danish raids of AD 884 and 1009 (report in preparation). Archaeological evidence relating to the medieval and early post-medieval periods is confined mainly to pottery and metalwork, associated with features such as ditches, pits and wells. Finds of clay pipes of south-western type attest to the role of Staines as a staging-post from the late 17th century (Barker 1976a).

II THE FRIENDS' BURIAL GROUND ('QUAKERS') SITE 1975–6: THE EXCAVATION

K R CROUCH and S A SHANKS

Introduction

In the early 19th century the Society of Friends purchased a site to the south of the High Street in Staines and built a new Meeting House, with adjoining burial ground, which was opened in 1844 (fig 14). The building was designed by Samuel Danvers in classical style (VCH 1962, 30). In all there were 78 graves, many of which contained more than one burial. The first interment was John Winstone in 1849, and the last Charles Ashby in 1944.

The Meeting House with part of its appurtenant land was sold in 1936, but the adjoining burial ground was retained, and a wooden Meeting House was erected south of the original building in 1937. The land was purchased by the Council in 1960 as part of their Central Redevelopment Scheme, and the burials were removed to a communal grave at Jordans Burial Ground in Buckinghamshire.

In 1970, two small trenches were opened by Mrs M Rendell at the south end of the site (fig 2), with the intention of determining the extent of the Roman settlement. The large amount of material recovered from so small an area posed many new problems, which it was felt could only be answered by further large-scale excavation.

The excavation

Work commenced in 1975 at the southern end of the site (fig 2), and despite the presence of several deep brick-lined graves, the levels proved in the main to be undisturbed. It was possible to define a sequence of prehistoric, Roman, Saxon, medieval and later occupation. In the lower levels, near to the water-table, the remarkably good preservation of iron, wood and other organic material provided additional information.

In the summer of 1976 the excavation of the northern end of the site, within the Roman town proper, produced evidence of Roman buildings, industrial activity, drainage and boundary ditches, with material indicating that Staines was a prosperous commercial centre.

Summary of features recovered

Geological features: feature nos 135, 158–9

Phase I: feature nos 241–8, 264–5, 270–5, 277–84
Mesolithic to Later Bronze Age (figs 3–4, 9, 15–18)

Prehistoric habitation on two islands, separated by water channels. Gradual silting up of these channels and expansion of occupation, especially in the Early to Middle Bronze Age.

Phase II: feature nos 264, 285
Later Bronze Age to Late Pre-Roman Iron Age (figs 3, 9, 59)

This phase was characterised by a yellow sandy clay deposit (285) sealing all lower levels, caused by a gradual rise in the water-table, leading to the flooding of the earlier occupation sites.

Phase III: feature nos 13, 88, 106, 138–40, 177, 180, 184, 188, 226, 249, 252–4, 256, 269, 285–6
Pre-Flavian (figs 5, 9)

Area now above water level; first Roman activity, consisting of ditch and bank delineating the area of later settlement.

Phase IV: feature nos 13, 49, 62–3, 83, 102, 189, 249, 252, 255–7, 289
Pre-Flavian (figs 5, 9)

Re-alignment of ditches and erection of a new clay bank system.

Phase V: feature nos 13, 63, 65, 89, 220, 227, 234, 249, 252, 258–9, 289
Pre-Flavian (figs 5, 9, 23)

Modification of ditch and bank system to include a revetment. Further activity within area enclosed by the ditches.

5

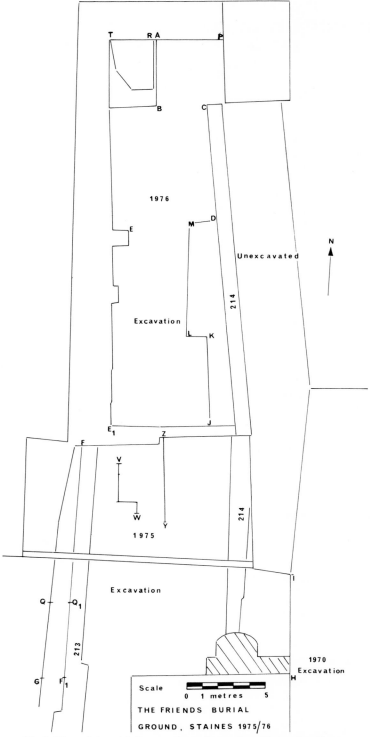

Fig 2. Plan of site with layout of trenches and positions of sections

Phase VI: feature nos 43, 108, 176
Pre- to early Flavian (figs 6-7, 23, 44, 48)
   Two large banks erected, overlying previous ditches and banks.

Phase VIA: feature nos 55, 81, 134, 225, 232, 260–2
Early Flavian (figs 6, 20, 23, 44, 48)
   Probably the end of the early phase of occupation on this site, with the levelling of the banks, and the cutting of small boundary-type ditches. Possibly pit 134 (burial) is also of this phase.

Phase VII: feature nos 14, 33, 42, 48, 56, 66–7, 69, 128–9, 144, 160, 167, 169, 181–2, 198, 231, 235, 238
Flavian to Hadrianic (figs 8–9, 11b, 12b, 20, 23–4, 35, 40–1, 43–4, 48, 56)
   First building on site, timber-framed with beam slot foundations. Associated boundary ditches, pits and pond. The building was dismantled *c* AD 130.

Phase VII/VIII: feature no 14
First half 2nd century (figs 8–9, 11b, 12b, 20, 24, 35, 41, 44, 48, 51, 53–5)
   Pond and later rubbish pit, in use in both periods.

Phase VIII: feature nos 14, 32, 34, 36–7, 40–1, 44–5, 48, 50–2, 54, 58, 60, 64, 68, 136–7, 142, 149–50, 166, 171–2, 178–9, 197, 230, 233, 239, 266, 270
Hadrianic to Antonine (figs 8–9, 11a–b, 12b, 20, 25–7, 33, 35–6, 40–1, 44, 48, 51, 53, 55, 56)
   Second larger building constructed with wooden beams of box-framed construction. Walls painted, evidence of tessellated pavement(s). Associated boundary ditches, and pits. Some reconstruction *c* AD 150/160.

Phase IX: feature nos 14, 30–1, 35, 70, 130, 133, 183, 187, 236
Antonine (figs 8–9, 11a, 12b, 21, 27–8, 33, 35, 41, 48, 53, 56)
   Reconstruction and contraction of second building. Pits indicative of industrial activity. Building deliberately dismantled at the end of this phase.

Phase IXA: feature nos 53, 191
Late Antonine (figs 8–9, 11a, 21, 28–9, 35–6, 40–4, 48, 51, 56)
   Levelling of site, layer containing much building debris.

Phase X: feature nos 29, 46–7, 57, 59, 80, 87, 89, 126–7, 141, 147, 155, 162, 164, 170, 173–5, 186, 190, 192, 212, 263, 267–8
Severan (figs 9–11b, 12b, 21, 29, 44, 48, 56)
   A timber building within a boundary ditch enclosure.

This building was burnt down early in the 3rd century, as shown by burnt daub and charcoal in the vicinity.

Phase XI: feature nos 9–10, 86, 90, 143, 204, 208
3rd century (figs 9, 11a–12a, 22, 30, 33, 35, 40–1, 43, 45, 49, 51, 53)
   Layers of flood debris and silt which sealed all earlier levels. Lapse in the occupation of the site spanning some 50 years.

Phase XII: feature nos 11, 16, 28, 71–5, 95–100, 105, 151, 218, 221
Late 3rd to early 5th centuries (figs 9–11b, 31–3, 41, 43, 45–6, 49, 51, 53, 55, 56)
   Black soil layer covering the site, cut by a rectangular ditched enclosure and two large pits, one of which was wood lined.

Phase XIII: feature nos 92, 117–18, 200–1, 203, 206–7, 211, 221–2, 237
5th to 7th centuries (figs 9–10, 11b–12a, 37, 47, 50)
   Part of a segmented gully system, of Saxon date, with associated industrial activity.

Phase XIV: feature nos 15, 20, 26, 223
7th to 8th centuries (figs 12b, 13, 46)
   Silt deposit from minor flooding, covering the southern end of the site. Square-cut pit and drainage channel at the north end of the site.

Phase XV: feature nos 5, 104, 109–14, 116, 119–21
8th to 11th centuries (figs 9, 11b–12a, 13, 37)
   Early medieval stone building with drainage channels and gravelled pathway. Associated pits and gullies.

Phase XVI: feature nos 1–4, 8, 17–19, 21–5, 38, 78, 82, 132, 202, 205, 215, 217, 290–6
12th to 14th centuries (figs 9, 11a–12b, 13, 33, 35–8, 41, 43, 46–7, 50–1, 53–4)
   Black soil layer and two pit groups.

Phase XVII: feature nos 8, 122
14th to 16th centuries (figs 9, 11a–12a, 14, 47, 50–1)
   Black soil layer sealing all the lower features.

Phase XVIII: feature nos 6, 7, 125
17th to 19th centuries (figs 9, 14, 39, 51)
   Three rubbish pits of early 19th century date.

Phase XIX: feature nos 39, 91, 93, 123–4, 195–6, 250–1
19th century (figs 9, 14)
   The foundation of the first Meeting House, which had built into it a brick-lined well, and adjoining graveyard. Also a large bottle pit.

Results of excavation

PHASE I, MESOLITHIC TO LATER BRONZE AGE (figs 3–4; 9; 15–18)

The evidence for two islands was found, separated by a 21m wide channel (270, Channel 1). Island 1 (271), at the northern end of the site, is presumably part of the main gravel island on which the modern town is centred. Island 2 (272), *c* 10m wide, was capped with a deposit of sandy clay (273), which formed a land surface in the late Neolithic and Early Bronze Age

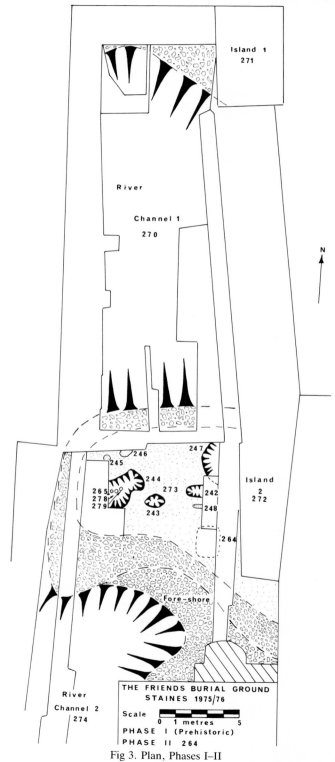

Fig 3. Plan, Phases I–II

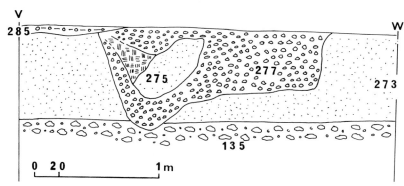

Fig 4. Section V–W (for the key, see fig 12c)

periods. There was a foreshore on the south-western side, *c* 4m wide, edging a further channel (274, Channel 2) into which Channel 1 probably drained.

The full depth and width of Channel 2 was never found, but a trench dug by machine *c* 15m south of Island 2 located the slope of the channel base at +10.62m OD, the full depth being at an unknown distance to the south. It is probable that during the Bronze Age Channel 1 was gradually filled by a deposit of sand, clay and silt (158). It may have become dry land, though still susceptible to flooding, so that occupation would have been restricted to the islands themselves.

Features of prehistoric date, probably the traces of habitation, were found on Island 2 (nos 242–8, 265, 278, 279). Due to disturbance by grave digging in the 19th century, no overall plan could be obtained. 244 was a large irregular oblong pit (3×2×0.45m) cut into the gravels and filled with clay (275) and gravel (277). This feature is possibly a Neolithic storage pit; a pit also cut into a gravel subsoil, with a similar section, was excavated at Pamphill, Dorset (Field *et al* 1964).

All other features, including the three post holes (265, 278, 279) which cut through 244 and into its base, are presumed to be Bronze Age. 245 (0.40×0.40×0.32m) and 246 (0.70×0.40×0.30m) were possible post holes, with a sandy/clay fill (280, 281) and were located to the north of 244. The three smaller possible post holes (265, 278, 279), each 0.20×0.20×0.53m, had a similar fill to those described above. Feature 243 (1.30×0.70×0.45m) had a clay fill (282) and lay to the south-east of 244.

The terminal ends of two features, 242 and 248, were sited to the east of these features and to the south of 247. 242 (0.80m wide and 0.23m deep) and 248 (0.30m wide and 0.18m deep) ran eastwards and both were filled with a single clay fill (283). Feature 247 (2.80×1.10×0.63m) is interpreted as part of a large circular hollow (perhaps a pit or hut) and had a single fill of orange clay (284).

PHASE II, LATER BRONZE AGE–LATE PRE-ROMAN IRON AGE (figs 3; 9; 59; pl 2)

This was a period of rising river levels, during which gravels, sands and clays (285) were deposited over Island 2 (272), filling and sealing the Bronze Age features discussed above. The only pre-Roman feature which cut into these layers was a roughly oval pit (264, 2×1.5×0.70m), in which was found the fully articulated skeleton of a cow, buried on its side, its skull turned back over the shoulder (fig 59 and pl 2). The true relationship of this feature to the stratigraphy of the site was difficult to establish, but a radiocarbon date, taken from the ribs, gives a date of *c* 870±100 bc.

PHASE III, ROMAN, PRE-FLAVIAN (figs 5; 9)

The first Roman features were two ditches (106, 226, 1.4m wide×0.50m surviving depth), both

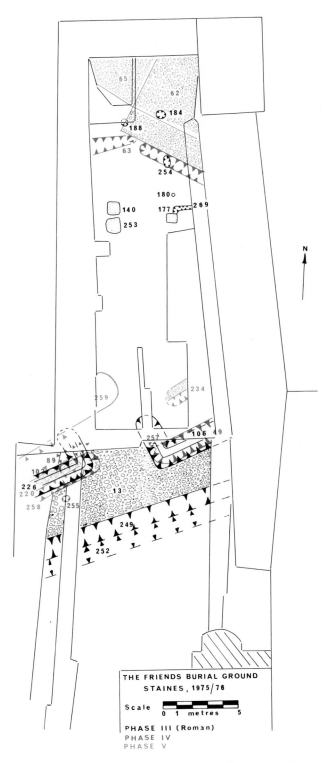

N

THE FRIENDS BURIAL GROUND
STAINES, 1975/76

Scale

0   1 metres   5

PHASE III (Roman)
PHASE IV
PHASE V

Fig 5. Plan, Phases III–V

with a square-cut basal channel (0.40×0.10m) filled with clean sand (88), later sealed by clay (256), and partly re-excavated to form the bank (83) for the ditch (102) of Phase IV. The orientation of the ditches was north-east–south-west along the northern slope of Island 2 (figs 3, 5). The two ditches turned northward and both probably terminated in a simple rounded end, the end of 106 being located during excavation. A gravelled area (13) lay between and south of the ditches. South of this again was a ditch (249) with a bank (252) on its southern side. The evidence for these last two features consisted principally of remains traced in the section (fig 9), the line of the ditch being almost obliterated by the cutting of later features. 13m north of ditches 106 and 226 a series of pits had been dug. Two pits (140 and 253, 0.70×0.70×0.25m) were square cut. 253 lay immediately south of 140 and contained the same fill of dark grey ashy soil (139) at the base, sealed by a mix of white clays and sands (138). 188 (0.30×0.30×0.35m), possibly a post hole, had a central fill of mixed soil and clay, surrounded by a gravel packing (285).

A single square-cut pit (177, 0.70×0.70×0.38m) had a drainage channel (269, 0.30×0.30×0.30m) leading from it, north-eastwards; both had a green sand fill (286). 180, 184 and 254 were all roughly circular features, possibly post holes. 180 (0.20×0.20×0.16m) and 184 (0.70×0.50×0.18m) had a fill of the same green sand as 177 and 269, whilst 254 (0.40×0.80×0.10m), of which only the very base survived, had a fill similar to 140 and 253.

Since no securely datable artefacts were found in any of these features, dating relies entirely upon the stratigraphy and the Flavian samian found in the bank (176, Phase VI) which sealed the features 140, 177 and 253.

PHASE IV, PRE-FLAVIAN (figs 5; 9)

Ditches 106 and 226 had silted up or had been filled in with clay (256) and new ditches with simple rounded ends (102 and 49, 1.5m wide and surviving depth 0.45m) were cut, following a slightly different alignment. The east ditch (49) had a small gully (257, 0.40m wide, 0.22m deep) feeding into it. In front of the west ditch (102), and cutting through the gravel (13) was a post hole (255, 0.50×0.50×0.25m deep). The clay silt (256) had been thrown up with the digging of 102 to form bank 289 (surviving height and width 0.40m). The ditch (249) and bank (252) south of the gravel surface (13) survived in this phase. Two possible post holes (184 and 188) were overlain by two small gullies (63, 0.80×0.40m deep, with clay fill 189) which in part delineated the extent of a gravelled area (62), edged with large flint pebbles. A date for this phase relies entirely upon stratigraphy and the evidence of the samian from the features of Phase VI.

The absence of closely datable material from phases III–IV may indicate intensive activity over a short period, or alternatively relatively little activity of a nature likely to leave artefacts.

PHASE V, PRE-FLAVIAN (figs 5; 9; 23, nos 1–5)

The ditches of Phase IV had an accumulation of gravel (227), whether deliberate or natural was difficult to establish, two new ditches were cut (258 and 234), and bank 289 was heightened. The westerly ditch (258) still followed the line of its predecessor, but the easterly ditch was aligned further north. 258 and 234 were 2×0.60m deep, and were divided longitudinally in half, probably by some form of wooden revetment, behind which gravel (220) had been packed (fig 9, A–F). There is some evidence for a third ditch (259, c 1.5m wide) behind ditch 258 and bank 289.

The ditch 249 and bank 252 were still in use, as were gullies 63, but the gravel area 62 had been made up and extended north-west (65). There were a few fragments of early Roman pottery from this phase, found lying on the surface of 65, including parts of a butt-beaker, but none of the pottery is closely datable.

PHASE VI, PRE- TO EARLY FLAVIAN (figs 6–7; 23, nos 6–8; 44, nos 1–2; 48, no 56)

During this phase a major reconstruction took place, as all previous features were filled in prior to the dumping of two areas of yellow sandy clay (43 and 108); in places dark stains were seen,

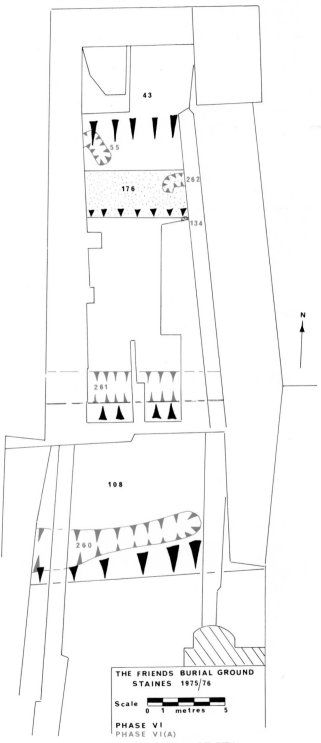

Fig 6. Plan, Phases VI–VIA

perhaps indicating the use of turf. The southern clay deposit (108) was *c* 10m wide and survived to an average thickness of 0.50m. Lying 13.50m north of it, clay deposit 43 was of similar make-up and was fronted by a sand bank (176, 3m wide), which contained early Flavian material.

PHASE VIA, EARLY FLAVIAN (figs 6; 20, no 1; 23, nos 9–18; 44, no 3; 48, no 55)

At the beginning of this phase two ditches were dug to the north and south of clay deposit 108. 260 (2.50m wide and 1m deep) and 261 (2m wide and surviving depth 0.50m) both had similar fills of brown pebbly soil (225 and 232). Cutting the northern clay deposit (43) and associated sand bank (176) were the ends of two curving ditches (55 and 262), both 1m wide, with a green sandy fill (81) topped by the brown pebbly soil (as 225 and 232). 134, a pit, contained eight near-complete vessels (fig 23, nos 9–15), including a samian bowl of form Ritterling 12, the flange of which had apparently been deliberately removed. It lay to the south of 262, and infant bones found in and around the feature may be associated with it. During the latter part of Phase VI or the beginning of Phase VIA, it would appear that clay deposits 43 and 108 were levelled, probably to allow for expansion of the settlement.

PHASE VII, FLAVIAN–HADRIANIC (figs 8–9; 11b;12b; 20, nos 2–4; 23–4, nos 19–47; 35, no 3; 40, no 5; 41, no 195; 43, nos 6, 9; 44, no 4; 48, nos 57–9; 56)

The remains of a timber-framed building were examined in this phase. A line of three rectangular post pits (48, 129, 235, all *c* 0.60×0.60×0.80m) was dug through the remains of the north clay deposit (43). These were linked by beam trenches (67 and 69, 2.0×0.30×0.30m) of a rectangular cut to carry timber 'sleeper' beams, with the wooden uprights sunk into the intervening pits. A third beam slot (144, of similar dimensions to 67 and 69) ran eastwards from 245. The end of a fourth beam slot (160) was seen in section. Against 67 and 129 a circular pit (66, *c* 1.30×0.90×0.35m) had been dug, which contained ash, slag, iron and bronze fragments.

South of pit 66 were four circular post holes (42, *c* 0.50×0.50m; 128, 0.85×0.80m; 194, 0.40×0.40m; and 198, 0.20×0.20m), all having similar fills of brown gravelly soil. Some 8m to

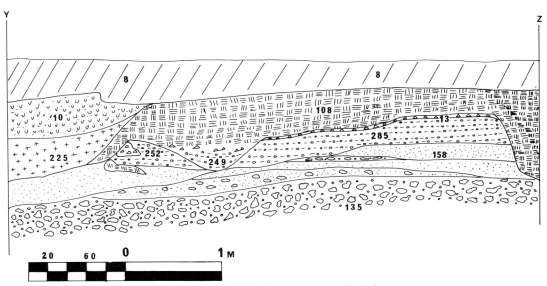

Fig 7. Section Y–Z (for the key, see fig 12c)

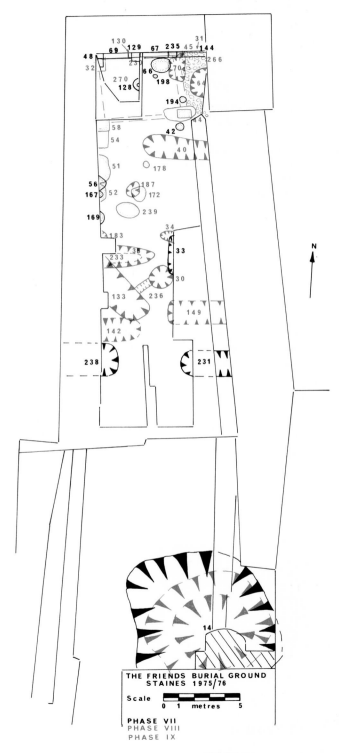

Fig 8. Plan, Phases VII–IXA

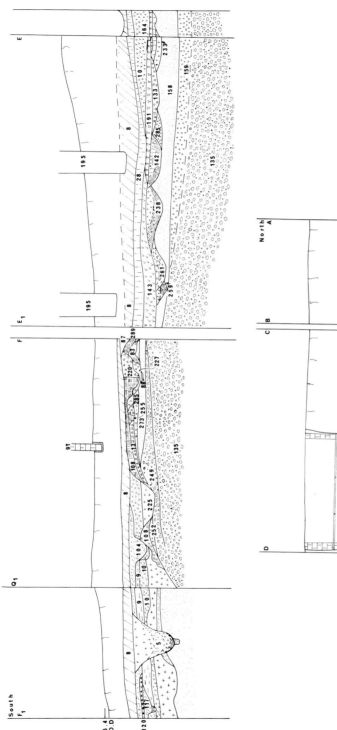

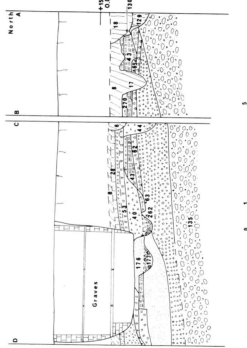

Fig 9. Composite section south–north across the site (for the key, see fig 12c)

the south was a series of features (56, 167 and 169) against the west baulk. The parts of these features which could be excavated measured 1m wide×0.30m deep (56), 0.40m wide×0.40m deep (167) and 0.85m wide×0.52m deep (169), but at no point was the full depth available for excavation. The edge of a further feature (33) lay to the south-east of the features above, and was 2.50m wide and 1.20m deep. All these had a green sandy fill (182) at the base, and the sides of the pits were undercut, which may have been caused by water being stored in them. A further 8m south the ends of two ditches were found (231, 1.70m wide×0.25m deep, and 238, 2.35m wide×0.73m deep), running parallel to the remains of the southern clay dump (108). Both of these ditches had a green fill similar to that of the above pits. South of the remains of the clay dump (108), a large, nearly circular pond (14, *c* 9×9×2m) had been dug (presumably fed by a spring located at the north-east corner during excavation), probably for the watering of livestock, as the edges were heavily pitted by what appeared to be hoof prints. By AD 120/30 the pond was being used as a rubbish tip. The final fill of all the above features, except the pond (14), was a brown stoney soil (181), and the samian found within them gave a *terminus post quem c* AD 130.

There was no evidence of the beams or posts of the building rotting *in situ,* and material recovered from the subsequent refilling with gravel of the post holes and beam slots gave a similar date to that of the final fill of the associated features. The nail graph (fig 57) shows a peak at *c* AD 130, and as the nails were bent or broken it would seem probable that at this time the building was demolished along with a general levelling of the site.

The material from the pond (14) is treated separately in the finds reports as *Phase VII/VIII* (figs 20, nos 5–19; 24, nos 48–56; 35, no 5; 41, nos 36, 128, 134; 44, nos 5–8; 48, nos 60–2; 51, nos 117, 122–3, 125–6, 128–34; 53, no 147; 54, nos 152, 154; 55, no 1).

PHASE VIII, HADRIANIC–MID ANTONINE (figs 8–9; 11a–b; 12b; 20, nos 20–36; 25–7, nos 57–122, 273; 33, no 266; 35, no 9; 36, no 269; 40, no 3; 41, nos 196, 198–200; 44, nos 9–12; 48, nos 63–5; 51, nos 115, 136; 53, no 145; 55, no 2; 56)

The beam slots and post holes of the previous phase were filled with gravel (266), to form a solid base for the erection of a new building. The post pits (32, 45 and 230) were recut close to the original line of the earlier building, these measuring 0.80×0.80×1.60m deep, 32 having a brown soil fill (148). Two new post pits (44 and 58) were dug to the south of pits 32 and 45. Pit 44 had a large square central shaft (*c* 0.90×0.90×2.5m deep) cut into a still larger pit (41, 2×1m). Pit 58 lay against the west baulk and measured *c* 0.80×0.60m.

Adjoining 58 was feature 54 (1.10m wide), possibly the cut to aid in the erection of a post in pit 58, both having a fill of dark brown ashy soil (60). The size of the post pits may be due to the nature of the subsoil, which is loose packed gravel, so that the sides of the pits were unstable and collapse of the sides caused the post pits to be much larger than needed. Inside the area outlined by the post pits a yellow clay floor (270) had been laid. In the northern section (fig 12b, A–P) were seen the remains of part of a daub wall (68, *c* 0.75m wide) which showed signs that it had been rendered with plaster and painted with a red ochre (plaster analysis by A Anderson, Leicester University). The presence of painted plaster and tesserae, together with window glass fragments, suggests a building of some substance.

To the east of the building lay a gravel surface (266) and cutting this was a shallow pit (64, 2m wide×0.21m deep). 1m to the south of the building had been dug a ditch (40, 1.50m wide×0.50m deep) which ran eastwards across the site, and a second one of the same dimensions (233) 6m south of 40, which ran in a westerly direction into the baulk. Ditch 233 had two main fills (37 and 36), 37 being a black soil and clay layer, and 36 a yellow clay and charcoal mix. Between the two ditches were cut a number of features (34, partly excavated, 0.85m wide; 51, partly excavated, 1.85m wide×0.30m deep; 52, partly excavated, 1.2m wide×0.30m deep; 172, 1×1×0.33m with a green sandy soil basal fill (171); and 178, 0.40×0.40×0.22m). Feature 239 (1×1.40×0.80m deep) lay 2m north of ditch 233, and had a primary fill of grey ashy soil (137). Above this lay a series of sand and clay lenses (50) with a final fill of black/brown ashy soil (136).

3.50m south of 233 lay ditches 142 and 149, both 0.60m wide and with a surviving depth of 0.45m, having a fill of green/yellow sand (166 and 150). Only the ends of these ditches lay within the area of the excavation, both having a similar final fill of black soil (179).

The pond (14) continued as a rubbish pit and had by now contracted in size to 8×6.50m; the fill of brown soil contained a large amount of pot and bone. The final fill of many of the above features was a brown soil (51 and 197) similar to that in the pond (14); it may have been a deliberate filling which would tie in with a possible change in the use of the area and a reconstruction of the building as suggested by the nail graph (fig. 57). The samian, colour-coated wares and other pottery evidence points to a date *c* AD 150/60 for the end of this phase.

PHASE IX, ANTONINE (figs 8–9; 11a; 12b; 21, nos 39–51; 27–8, nos 123–56, 274; 33, no 259; 35, nos 7, 10; 41, no 140; 48, no 68; 53, no 144; 56)

Evidence for a modification to the Phase VIII building comes from several factors. Feature 70 (1.90×1×0.45m) overlay 45, post pit 230 showed signs of having been recut (130) and a new clay floor (31) was laid to the east (seen only in section: fig 12b). 13m south of the building lay ditch 133 (2m wide with a surviving depth of 0.30m). It was orientated from north-west to south-east and had been dug over the remains of ditch 233. Alongside ditch 133 was a circular pit (30, 1.50×1.50×0.70m); this pit had a fill of black ashy soil containing the remains of at least 25 cow skulls and a large amount of pottery. Leading into ditch 133 was a small gully (236, 0.50m wide, 0.15m deep) which probably connected pit and ditch, though this could not be proved in excavation. Two other features were located between 133 and the building: 183, of which no useful dimensions were obtainable, and 187 (0.90×1×0.34m), both having a brown clay fill (185).

During this phase the fill of ditch 233 settled and the resultant depression was filled with a brown ashy soil (35), as outlined on fig 8. The pond (14), now contracted to *c* 5×5m, continued in use as a rubbish dumping area until the end of the phase.

Material from the fill of post pit 130 and the other features gives a *terminus post quem* of AD 180/90. The absence of any sign of the posts of this modified building rotting *in situ* suggests that it had been deliberately dismantled at this time, much of its debris being found in the succeeding layer. Further confirmation of demolition comes from the nail graph (fig 57).

PHASE IXA, LATE ANTONINE (figs 8–9; 11a; 21, nos 52–62; 28–9, nos 157–77; 35, no 2; 36, no 270; 40, no 6; 41, no 197; 42; 43, no 1; 44, nos 13–18; 48, no 69; 51, nos 118–19, 137; 56; pl 1)

Sealing the features and structures of Phase IX were contemporary layers (53 and 191), consisting of a dark ashy soil, with charcoal, daub, tile, pottery and bone in large quantities, all in a 'fresh' condition, and showing little signs of abrasion. A date of *c* AD 180/90 is suggested by the pottery.

PHASE X, SEVERAN (figs 9–11b; 12b; 21, nos 66–72; 29, nos 178–89; 44, nos 19–20; 48, no 75; 56)

Bounding the northern edge of the remains of the southern clay dump (108) of Phase VI were the ends of two ditches (80, 1.50m wide×0.50m deep; 87, 1.50m wide×0.50m deep). Ditch 80 had a small square-cut channel (89) along its base (0.30m wide×0.20m deep) and it is probable that 87 was similarly cut. The fill of both was a brown/black soil, charcoal flecked, with daub and burnt pot. At the end of 80 was a small stake hole (267, 0.10×0.10m) and a post hole (268, 0.30×0.30m), both having a brown soil fill. 1.50m north of ditch 87 was a second post hole (126, 0.40×0.40m) which had a black soil fill (127). 13m north of these ditches lay parts of a beam slot (164 and 170) which were 0.30m wide and 0.20m deep, and cut the edge of a laid clay surface (190). This complex was possibly the remains of a building with a clay floor, its entrance being in the north-west corner (2m wide). Much of the building had been destroyed by later activity, but the presence of a gravelled surface (162) outside another beam slot (155, 0.30×0.20m) allows for a calculation of a structure some 6.50×9m. North of the entrance to the building a line of pits had been dug (59, 186 and 173), all *c* 0.70×0.70×0.30m and having a similar fill of brown powdery soil and ash. Leading away from the edge of pit 186 was a series of stake holes all *c* 0.20m in diameter. The alignment of the stake holes (57, 147, 263, 47 and 46) was northward for 9.50m, then turned eastwards for a further 2.50m, before disappearing into the baulk. 1m north of 173, lay a shallow gully or pit (175, 0.50m wide×0.30m deep) which ran eastwards and had a green clay basal fill (192) and a top fill of brown soil (174). Layers 29 and 141 covered the clay floor 190, and were themselves a mixture of clay, soil, charcoal and daub, which, together with burnt material from ditches 80 and 87 and a burnt area (212), suggest that the structure may have burnt down. A probable date for this phase is early in the 3rd century, indicated by a coin of Caracalla in pit 59, and by the pottery.

PHASE XI, 3RD CENTURY (figs 9; 11a–12a; 22, no 100; 30, nos 190–209; 33, nos 260, 265; 35, nos 1, 4, 8, 11; 40, no 1; 41, nos 1, 8, 129, 136, 202; 43, nos 4–5, 8, 10; 45, nos 21–5; 49, nos 76–87; 51, no 120; 53, no 148)

This phase was characterised by a sequence of flood deposits. The first (10 and 143) was a mix of soils, clays and sands, with much pottery, slightly abraded, bone and tile; the second was of muddy silts (86, 90, 204 and 208) which, with a clean green silt (9), overlay 10 at the southern end of the site. 10 and 143 were seen as a deposit overlying 14, banking up against 108, and lying between 108 and 176. The second deposit overlay 10 south of 108, and there the combined depth of all the deposits reached a maximum of 2.10m (fig 11b). 9 only occurred beyond the southern edge of 108, presumably indicating that the area was under water, while the northern part of the site was relatively dry. The pottery within 10 cannot be dated much later than the early 3rd century. The depositional character of 9 and 10 would seem to suggest formation under flood conditions, 10 being the result of an initial flood surge, and 9 a quiet period, allowing the accumulation of more than 1m of silts (fig 11b).

The length of time during which this flooding affected the site can only be estimated, as conditions while excavating did not allow for detailed analysis. The pottery and coin evidence suggest that the area was abandoned from *c* AD 220 to 250/70. It is a matter of conjecture whether flooding was the sole cause of this abandonment or combined with as yet unknown factors.

PHASE XII, LATE 3RD CENTURY TO EARLY 5TH CENTURY, figs 9–11b; 31–2, nos 210–58; 33, no 267; 41, nos 5–7, 42, 127, 137, 184, 194, 201; 43, nos 12, 14; 45, nos 26–33; 46, nos 30, 34; 49, nos 88–100; 51, nos 121, 124, 127; 53, nos 146, 149; 55, no 3; 56)

Following Phase XI there was a build up of black soil over the site. Different sequences were observed north and south of the line of the former bank 108. 28 lay north of 108 and is dated mid/late 3rd century–early 5th century. 16 lay south of 108 and dated from the early 4th century to the 5th century. This suggests that the area to the south was still marshy until the 4th century. Dating depends upon the pottery, coins and small finds found within 28 and 16.

A rectangular ditched enclosure (11, 6.70m wide) was found within the build up of black soil 28. The ditches were 1m wide×0.75m deep, with a 'V' section, and a fill of black/grey fibrous soil (151). In the base of the western ditch was the bottom half of a large greyware storage vessel from the Farnham/Alice Holt area, cut down to form a large bowl, containing all the fragments of a late 3rd/4th century Verulamium jar, which at the time of deposition may have been intact (fig 32, no 239; see pottery report, Fabric H, for discussion of a late date for pottery produced in the Verulamium region).

With these two vessels of typical Roman manufacture in ditch 11 were the fragments of several hand-made, shell-tempered vessels (fig 32, no 241). Outside the south-west corner of the ditched enclosure (11) was a shallow pit (71, 1×1×0.24m) filled with charcoal and iron slag. Two stake holes were found on the north and south edges of 71 (73 and 74, 0.60×0.11×0.10m). To their south-west was a third (75, 0.07×0.08×0.75m), which at some time had been recut (218), and

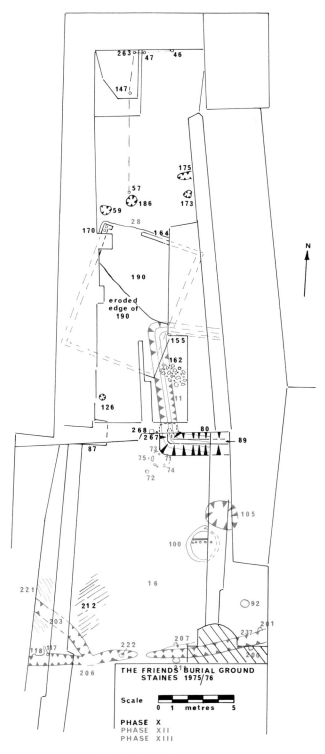

Fig 10. Plan, Phases X, XII–XIII

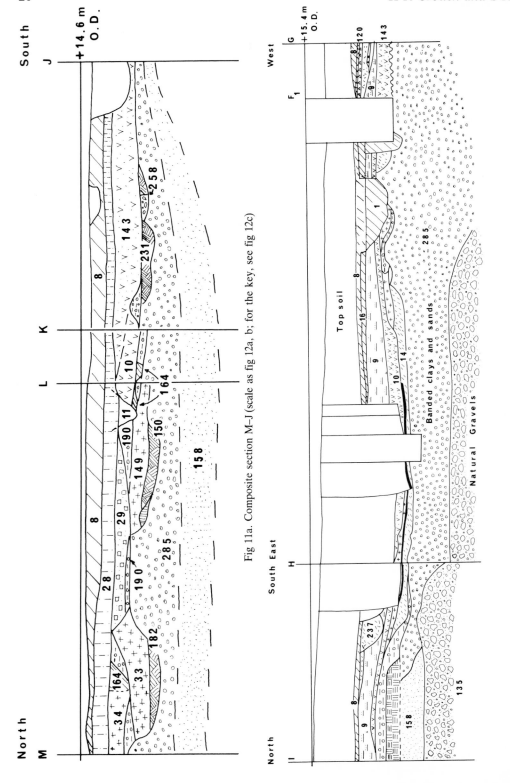

Fig 11a. Composite section M–J (scale as fig 12a, b; for the key, see fig 12c)

Fig 11b. Composite section I–G (for the key, see fig 12c)

south of stake hole 75 was a fourth (72, 0.20×0.20×0.10m). Directly south of 11 lay two large circular pits, 100 (1.9×1.9×2m) and 105 (2.1×1.9×2m) which cut, in part, 9 and 108. These two pits were dug along the line of the spring which had fed the pond (14) and it is probable that they were wells. 100 had been partly wood lined and five wooden stakes of pollarded oak edged the remains of a wooden plank (wood identified by Mrs A Locker, Ancient Monuments Laboratory). There were six layers within the pit (in ascending order, 221, 99, 98, 97, 96 and 95). 221 was a gravel, 99 a black clay, 98 a grey muddy clay, 97 a red brown soil, 96 a green clay, from which a rim of a shell-tempered vessel was recovered (fig 32, no 240), and 95 a black soil, which may be interpreted as part of layer 16, which sealed these features, and contained late Roman pottery and a number of shell-tempered vessels (fig 32, nos 242–58). Pit 105 contained the body sherds of a 4th century Farnham/Alice Holt storage jar. Within both pits were found limestone blocks, daub and ash; an explanation as to why the lining of pit 100 was seemingly never completed could be that a nearby structure, with which the two wells were associated, had burnt down and some of the debris from it been thrown into these two pits/wells. It may be that the building destroyed lay within the ditched enclosure 11.

PHASE XIII, 5TH–7TH CENTURIES (figs 9–10, 11b–12a; 37, no 5; 47, no 45; 50, no 106)

The features of this phase were found bordering the southernmost edge of the site. 237 and 206 were interpreted as part of a segmented gully system (0.70×0.70m deep) that ran east–west across the site. Along their edges were cut a number of post holes (207, 211, 200, 201) and set into the end of one (206) was a further post hole (222); all had a diameter of 0.30m. All the gullies and post holes were filled with a green silt (223; see below, Phase XIV).

Running into the western segment of the gully system from a north-westerly direction was a third gully, 203 (0.70m wide×0.50m deep). Running into 206 was a small gully (117, 0.20m wide×0.20m deep), and where it entered gully 206 was a post hole (118, 0.10m diam×0.25m deep) with a gravel packing containing iron slag and wood fragments. On the eastern side of the site 2m north of 237 was a circular pit (92, 0.50×0.50×1m), which was steep-sided and flat-bottomed, containing charred material near its top. North of 203, and cut by it, was an area of black soil (221, perhaps part of 16). All these features contained very worn fragments of Roman pottery, with handmade grass-tempered pottery typical of the early Saxon period.

PHASE XIV, 7TH–8TH CENTURIES (figs 12b; 13; 46, no 41)

The features of Phase XIII were filled and covered by a silt deposit (223), which was probably formed as a result of flooding. At the far north of the site there was evidence of human activity. A rectangular pit (20, part excavated 1.30×0.20m) cut the black soil 28 and earlier Roman features. Only half of this pit was excavated, as the rest lay outside the area of excavation. To the south-west of 20 was a post hole (26, 0.27×0.27×0.15m), and a small slot or channel (15) ran from it (0.10×0.30m); both were filled with a black soil. A probable date for these features is Saxon, the result of a transfer of occupation northwards when the area to the south became unsuitable for habitation due to flooding.

PHASE XV, 8TH–11TH CENTURIES (figs 9; 11b–12a; 13; 37, nos 1–4, 7, 9–12)

The southern part of the site was reoccupied during this phase. A building with flint pebble footings (111, 1m wide) was constructed south of the earlier Saxon gullies (237 and 206). Only the north-west corner of this building was available for excavation. In the centre of the excavated part of the foundations was a post hole (112, 0.40×0.40×0.20m) and within the building was a clay floor (114). From the corner of the building, running north-west, was a steep-sided, flat-bottomed channel (109, 0.90m wide×0.30m deep), probably for drainage, as it sloped away from the building. Part of the wall of the building survived on the western side, represented by a mix of tile, stone and brown clay (113). Here a second drainage channel (110, 0.70m wide) led

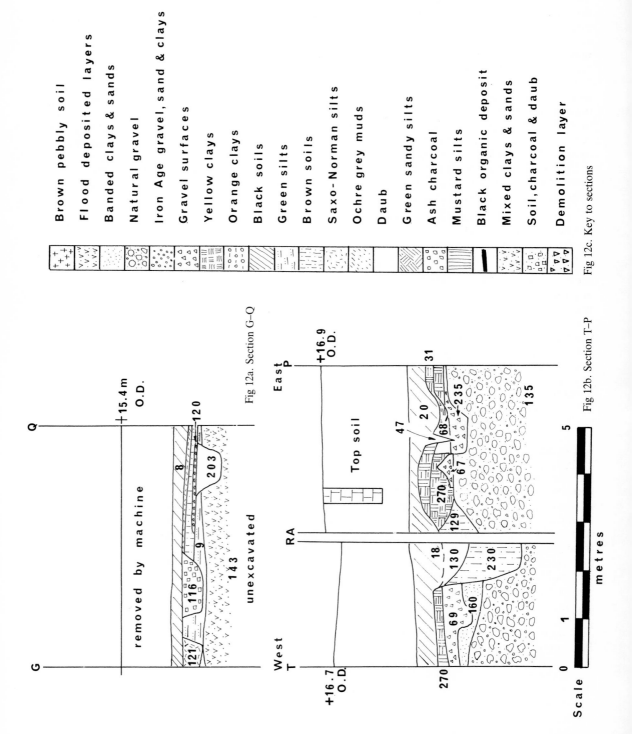

Brown pebbly soil
Flood deposited layers
Banded clays & sands
Natural gravel
Iron Age gravel, sand & clays
Gravel surfaces
Yellow clays
Orange clays
Black soils
Green silts
Brown soils
Saxo-Norman silts
Ochre grey muds
Daub
Green sandy silts
Ash charcoal
Mustard silts
Black organic deposit
Mixed clays & sands
Soil, charcoal & daub
Demolition layer

Fig 12a. Section G–Q

Fig 12b. Section T–P

Fig 12c. Key to sections

away from this wall westwards. A gravelled path (120, 1m wide) led northward for 8m. North of it lay the end of a feature (104) draining westwards, which at the baulk was 1m wide and 0.50m deep.

Path (120) had been cut by two features, 5 and 116. Only a small part of 5 survived; it was a pit with a square cut base (2.0m diam×1.75m deep) and had 5 layers: in ascending order, brown soil (76), green sandy silt (77), brown pebbly soil (84), brown soil (85) and brown pebbly soil (101). 116 was a roughly squared pit (1.40m wide×0.40m deep) filled with a purple/brown soil with charcoal and slag. In the base of this pit were fragments of wood, suggesting that it may have had a wooden lining. A further rectangular feature (121, 0.70m wide×0.50m deep) lay to the south of 116. It had been cut into the line of the earlier gully, 206, and its fill was gravel (119) at the base, sealed by a black charcoal soil. This shallow receptacle also appeared to have been wood lined, a dark stained edge and wood fragments being noted.

This building and associated features were probably Saxo-Norman in date, as they were cut by a series of pits of the late 12th/13th centuries (see below, Phase XVI).

PHASE XVI, 12TH–14TH CENTURIES (figs 9; 11a–12b; 13; 33, nos 262–4; 35, no 6; 36, no 272; 37, nos 6, 8, 13–25; 38, nos 26–31; 41, no 203; 43, nos 15–17; 46, nos 35–8, 40, 42; 47, nos 46–7; 50, nos 107–13; 51, no 116; 53, no 150; 54, no 153)

This phase was characterised by two areas of pit digging, one at the extreme north, and one at the south of the site. The southern group of three circular pits with squared bases (1, 2 and 3) cut the building and associated features of Phase XV, described above. 1 (2.30×1.60m deep) had a fill in the base of dark grey clay, mixed with the underlying sands (290). Sealing this, in turn, were a grey/brown clay (291) and a dark grey/black deposit (292), with occasional building material and Roman and medieval pottery fragments.

Only a quarter of pit 2 was excavated and it had a similar construction to 1. The initial fill (217) was a peaty organic deposit, which was progressively darker towards the base. This was sealed by a greeny/brown fill (215), with occasional Roman and medieval pottery sherds, sealed in turn by a brown soil (132) with a few pebbles and medieval potsherds. Pit 3 was again similar to pit 1, 2m wide×1.80m deep. The initial fill was a mixture of orange/yellow clay with a black mud (293), this mix being from the wall of the pit, which had been undercut at this depth. Above was a layer of thick black mud (294), covered by a black ashy soil and charcoal (295). The final fill was a fine black soil (296). Cutting the corner of 2 was an edge of a fourth pit (202), possibly similarly constructed to those described above. The date of these pits is probably 13th century, according to the pottery recovered from them.

At the northern end of the site was a series of pits and post holes. Feature 18 was part of a shallow pit (1.70×0.50×0.20m) with a fill of black soil; 0.50m north-east of it was a second elliptical pit (21, 1.48×0.96×0.31m), also with a black soil fill. Cutting the western edge of 21 was a post hole (4, 0.20×0.20×0.30m). Directly south of pit 18 lay a third oval pit (17), most of which lay beneath the baulk, filled with black soil similar to that in 18 and 21. Lying 1m east of 17, and approximately 1m south of 21, was a large subrectangular pit (22, 1.73×1.62×0.50m), with two post holes at the northern corners (78, 82, 0.22×0.22×0.31m). A ledge 0.17m down, ran round three sides of the pit. The fill of pit 22 was again black soil containing Roman and medieval pottery sherds. Flanking it to the east and west were four post holes (19, 23, 24 and 25, each 0.20×0.20×0.04m); since only the very bases of these post holes were present, it is difficult to determine whether they were part of the pit complex. Their dating is tenuous, but since there was very little evidence of later medieval activity, they have been assigned to this phase. 6m south of this complex lay a single rectangular pit (38, 0.40×0.90×0.80m) with a fill of black soil containing medieval pottery and a 13th century prophylactic glass vessel (fig 41, no 203). Between the northern and southern groups of pits and overlying them was a black soil 8. The material recovered from this layer could be dated Saxo-Norman to 15th century and presumably it must therefore represent several phases, both cut by and sealing the above mentioned features.

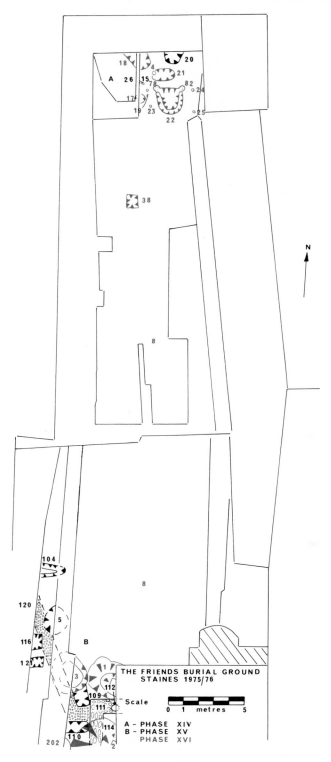

Fig 13. Plan, Phases XIV–XVI

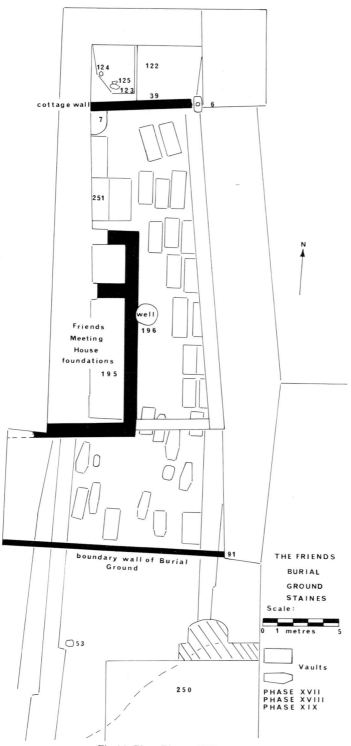

Fig 14. Plan, Phases XVII–XIX

PHASE XVII, 14TH–16TH CENTURIES (figs 9; 11a–12a; 14; 47, nos 48–9; 50, no 114; 51, no 139)

This phase was primarily represented by the black soil layer 122. The differentiation between 122 and 8 was only possible at the very north of the site where there had been no later disturbance of the upper soil layers by grave digging.

Pottery from the layer was of all periods up to the 16th century, together with bone and building material.

PHASE XVIII, 17TH–19TH CENTURIES (figs 9; 14; 39; 51, nos 140–3)

Three pits (6, 7 and 125) contained pottery of late 18th to early 19th century date, and two coins of George III. Pit 6 was a wide, shallow, rectangular depression, with a central shaft (1.10×0.50m); the top fill consisted of gravel and pottery, and the shaft contained a mixture of soil and bottle glass. Pit 7 was apparently a large circular pit, the section excavated being 1.11×1.14×0.60m. The base layer of the pit was made up of wood shavings; a folding bone penknife, bone comb and a button were found amongst them. The general filling was a mixture of soil, building brick, pottery and glass. Pit 125 was a small rectangular hollow (0.20×0.30×0.20m) containing sherds of post-medieval pottery similar to that from 6 and 7. Fragments of pottery from all three pits have been found to join and this suggests a contemporary date for all three. These three pits were partly or wholly sealed beneath the 19th century cottage (see fig 14). Due to the heavy disturbance of the rest of the site by the grave digging and later mechanical excavation of the graveyard, there was no evidence of other features which could be associated with this phase. It is possible that the black soil 122 continued through this phase but there was no definite evidence of it having done so.

PHASE XIX, 19TH CENTURY (figs 9; 14)

This phase covers the period during which the site belonged to the Society of Friends. The foundations of the eastern wall of the Friends' Meeting House (195), constructed 1843/44 and opened 18 July 1844, which were of concrete, lay along the western side of the site. An integral part of the wall was a brick-lined well (196, 4.0m deep×1.40m wide), which had been capped by a 1m thick deposit of lime (a commonly found feature of 18th/19th century wells throughout the town). 7m to the south of the Meeting House was the boundary wall of the Burial Ground (91). A cottage was built at the same time as the Meeting House at the northern end of the site, the foundations (39) sealing pits 6, 7 and 125.

Thirty-four graves were excavated, of which 31 were brick-lined and had been used for up to four burials, one upon the other, separated by a flagstone floor, with an average size of 2–2.5m long, 1m wide and 1.5–2.5m deep. The base of one such vault (251) showed modification to take a child burial. Either wood or lead coffins were used with brass handles and fittings: the handles showed many variations in design (these fittings have been retained for possible future study). Some of the burials had been placed in shallow graves between the brick vaults.

The land immediately to the south of the burial ground wall belonged to the Ashby family and the huge pit (250) was used by them to dump broken bottles and other rubbish from their bottling plant. Several other pits of 19th century date were found, containing building rubble (93, 123 and 124).

III THE FINDS

The flints

PHILIP JONES
figs 15–17

This report was completed by 1979, and therefore does not take account of subsequent research.

Richard Bradley, of the University of Reading, has kindly commented on a draft of the flint report.

The catalogue of flints is on microfiche 1–5

A total of 188 worked flints was recovered in the 1975/6 excavations, and of these 115 were retouched and a further 16 showed some signs of use. The remaining waste material was mainly the by-products of blade production. Most of the flints were pale grey/buff to dark grey or black in colour, typical of nodular flints derived from the Upper Chalk, and only 18 flints were of a different colour that might indicate another source, probably the local river gravels. Despite their presence as residual material in Roman and later levels, only a few of the flints were rolled, and only 34 retouched flakes and blades had been damaged beyond recognition of their type.

The long sequence of prehistoric pottery from the Friends' Burial Ground is complemented by the worked flints recovered as residual material in Roman and later levels. There is little that can be directly attributed to the Later Bronze Age, most of the mixed assemblage being of either Mesolithic, Neolithic or earlier Bronze Age types and techniques. The Mesolithic forms probably include the three small blade cores and the four or five microliths, whilst the utilised and retouched blades, which make up more than half of all the finished products found on the site, could be of Mesolithic or Neolithic date. Burins, and even some microlith types, sometimes continued as a small part of Neolithic assemblages (Wainwright 1972), but it seems more likely that there was some Mesolithic settlement in the area of what is now the High Street. Earlier Neolithic occupation is indicated by the leaf arrowhead (fig 17, no 30), many of the scrapers and awls, and the production of small blades.

Some distinct types can be isolated from the mixed assemblage as being representative of the late Neolithic/earlier Bronze Age. Bifacially worked, plano-convex, and polished-edge knives (fig 17, no 37), as well as the two barbed and tanged arrow-heads, are all typical of the later 3rd and early 2nd millennium BC, having been found associated with Beakers, Grooved Ware or Early Bronze Age pottery in southern England (Wainwright & Longworth 1971; Piggott 1954, 183; Sieveking 1968, 77). However, since only five possibly Neolithic to Early Bronze Age sherds have been identified by Barrett (fig 18, nos 1–5) there remains the possibility that more of the less proficiently made flints may belong to the Later Bronze Age than might have been considered likely without the evidence of the pottery. The possibility of settlement (or perhaps even burials) on the Staines gravel islands during the early 3rd millennium BC remains an open question, but with so much later occupation and river erosion there is little concrete evidence for settlement other than finds in the general vicinity.

From the evidence of Later Bronze Age settlements, it is clear that the standards of flint-working, the range of types and the quantity of such assemblages, declined as the utilisation of certain metal forms became more widespread (Cunliffe & Phillipson 1968, 226; Rahtz & Apsimon 1962, 323). Apart from the continued use of scrapers, flints became mere tools-of-the-moment to be selected and used without much further modification, and discarded after use. Some of the earlier lithic material such as the polished-edge knife (fig 17, no 37) gained fresh usage after its initial loss by the working of a steep scraping edge along one broken facet.

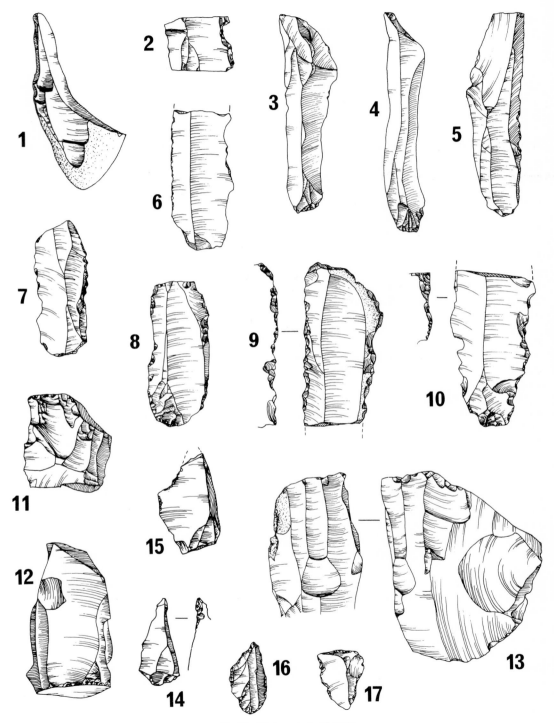

Fig 15. Flints, nos 1–17 (1/1)

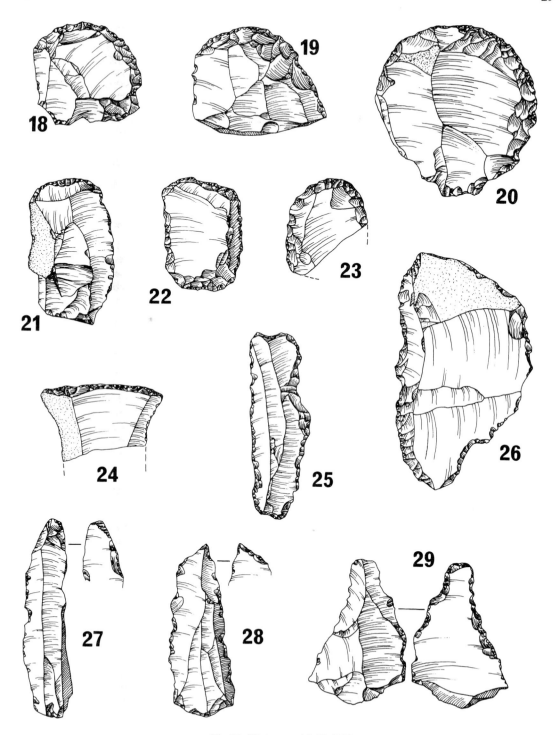

Fig 16. Flints, nos 18–29 (1/1)

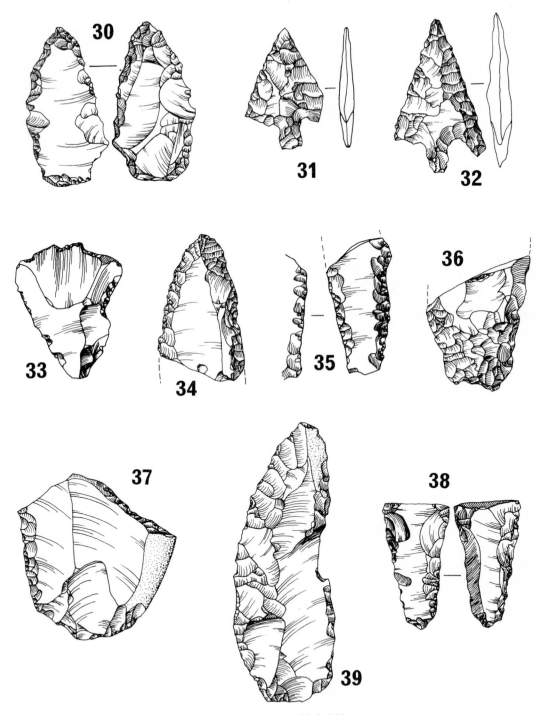

Fig 17. Flints, nos 30–9 (1/1)

This modification could have occurred during the earlier Bronze Age but the difference of patina on the re-worked edge may indicate a Later Bronze Age dating.

Good quality flint (not derived from the local gravels) was introduced to the site for the production of these blades and flake tools. Both the Thames and the Colne river systems pass through the Upper Chalk from which flint derives as tabular strata, or as nodules in horizontal seams. It is predominantly black to pale blue-grey in colour with a thick white to buff cortex, and is relatively devoid of the internal fractures seen in glacial or alluvial gravels. The nearest outcrop of the Upper Chalk is at Windsor Castle, 7km upstream of Staines.

The prehistoric pottery

JOHN C BARRETT

fig 18

This report was completed by 1979 and therefore does not take account of subsequent research.

David Longley and Martin O'Connell, of the Surrey Archaeological Unit, and Stuart Needham, of the British Museum, have kindly provided information.

The catalogues of fabrics and vessels are on microfiche 6–9.

Discussion

A long, albeit intermittent, sequence of activity is represented by this group of prehistoric pottery, extending from the Middle Neolithic to Late pre-Roman Iron Age.

Three sherds (fig 18, nos 1–3) may be tentatively assigned to a series of open bowls with rolled rims whilst a fourth (fig 18, no 4) may be from a similar bowl form. Such vessels would belong to the ceramic traditions of the southern British Middle Neolithic, although it is impossible to assign this material to any particular style zone within these traditions. An important assemblage of material of this period has recently been recovered on the southern bank of the Thames at Runnymede Bridge, Egham (Longley & Needham 1979). Downstream Middle Neolithic settlement on the flood plain of the Thames is also attested at Putney, with other finds coming from Twickenham, Brentford and Fulham (Warren 1977). A fuller understanding of the period in this area must await the publication of the excavations of the Staines causewayed camp (Robertson Mackay 1962).

By far the largest group of prehistoric pottery from the site belongs to the Bronze Age. One sherd (fig 18, no 5) is decorated with twisted cord impressions, this being one of four sherds belonging to fabric group 1. This fabric and the use of cord impressions are diagnostic of many classes of Early Bronze Age urn, including biconical and collared urns. This decorated sherd may represent the latter class of vessel. Those collared urns which are known from the middle reaches of the Thames valley are mainly derived from burial contexts (Gardner 1924, 6). However, the Staines sherds, a sherd in a similar fabric from Petters Sports Field, Egham (excavations by B Johnson), and perhaps the similar material reported from the City of London (pers comm B Hobley), suggest that such material might also be encountered in settlement contexts in this region. Other urn material may be represented by fabric group 9.

The main class of Bronze Age pottery on this site belongs to the Deverel–Rimbury tradition. This includes bucket urns in the coarse fabric group 2. These vessels may be decorated along the top of the rim (fig 18, nos 6–8) or have plain rims (fig 18, no 9). Other decoration includes finger-tip impressions around the girth of the vessel and the use of applied cordons (fig 18, nos

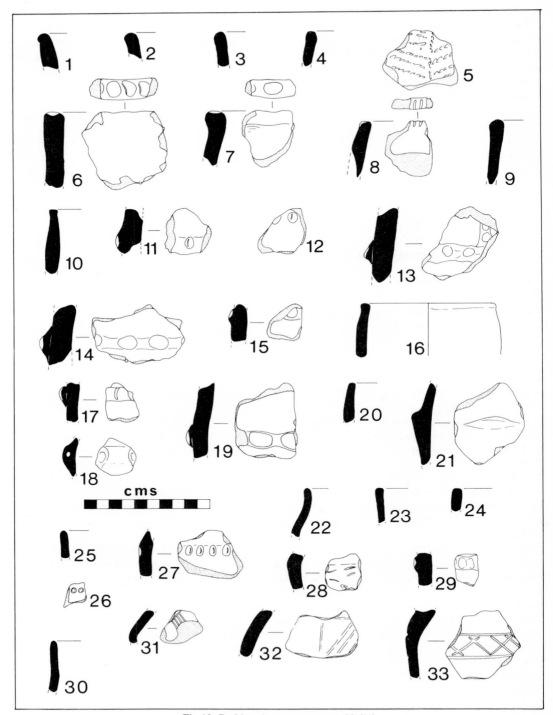

Fig 18. Prehistoric pottery, nos 1–33 (⅓)

11–15, 17, 19). The latter technique includes the relatively elaborate motif of a 'horse-shoe' band (fig 18, no 13) which occurs again locally in the cremation cemetery at Sunbury (Barrett 1973, fig 1, no 1). Also included in this tradition are globular urns (fig 18, nos 10, 18, 20, 21) and a small tub-like vessel (fig 18, no 16). The latter is comparable to the slightly larger vessel from Sunbury (Barrett 1973, fig 2, no 18). The globular vessels occur in finer and better fired fabrics than the bucket urns. These vessels are undecorated although two lugs are represented, one of which is horizontally perforated. Decorated globular vessels are known from Sunbury (Barrett 1973, fig 2, nos 15, 16) and from the recently excavated settlement site at Muckhatch Farm, Thorpe, Surrey (Johnson 1975, 19). An undecorated globular vessel was found at Yiewsley (Barrett 1973, fig 5, no 2).

Although customarily assigned to the Middle Bronze Age (*c* 1400–1100 BC) the Deverel–Rimbury tradition may have much earlier origins in the Early Bronze Age (Barrett 1976). The occurrence of this occupation debris at Staines can now be set against other occupation material in the area, including the site at Muckhatch Farm, Thorpe, early material from Petters Sports Field, Egham, and the probable storage vessels from Kempton Park (Sheppard 1975). This evidence for occupation accords well with the cemetery finds from the middle reaches of the Thames, cemeteries whose distribution shows a marked concentration in the west London area (Barrett 1973, fig 7).

In the three centuries following the end of the Deverel–Rimbury tradition a distinctive 'post-Deverel–Rimbury' ceramic tradition is found in most areas in southern Britain. Although clearly represented in the middle reaches of the Thames, with an important assemblage recently discovered at Runnymede Bridge (Longley 1976), such material is not obviously represented at Staines, with perhaps one exception (fig 18, no 22). However, the pottery styles which originate in the 8th century BC are represented here. These are marked by an increased use in decoration when compared with the earlier material, and such styles seem to run from the 8th to 5th centuries BC.

An important assemblage has recently been excavated at Petters Sports Field, Egham, where the pottery was found to be overlying a hoard of Later Bronze Age metalwork (O'Connell & Needham 1977). The metalwork includes Carps Tongue and Ewart Park material which might well indicate an 8th century date of deposition. Fabric group 5 from Staines is defined partly by its distinctive sandy feel, and sandy fabrics are well represented amongst the Petters Sports Field material. This fabric group includes a jar decorated with finger-tip impressions around the shoulder and another jar which has fingernail impressions on the body of the vessel (fig 18, nos 27, 28). Both forms of decoration find general comparison amongst the Petters Sports Field assemblage (O'Connell & Needham 1977, fig 5, nos 1, 3, 4). Staines has also produced a sherd bearing an applied cordon decorated with finger-tip impressions, a form of decoration which continues amongst material of this general date. Three plain rims also derive from coarse jars (fig 18, nos 23–25). Finer decorated vessels are also represented, the sherds coming either from bowls (fig 18, nos 26, 31) or from a finer decorated jar (fig 18, no 32). One other rim sherd comes from a bowl (fig 18, no 30).

Finally there is the decorated sherd in the distinctive shelly fabric of fabric group 6 (fig 18, no 33); although difficult to parallel, it is likely that such a sherd would date to the later part of the Iron Age.

Conclusions

All the pottery discussed above had been redeposited in Roman features, but must represent debris from substantial earlier settlement in the immediate vicinity (see site report, Phase I). These finds, when placed in their immediate setting, indicate the importance of Neolithic settlement along the reaches of the middle Thames. They also bear further witness to extensive and long-lived activity in this region during the Bronze Age.

Samian wares

GEOFF MARSH
figs 19–22

These reports were completed by 1979, and therefore do not take account of subsequent research.

The report on the stamps was kindly provided by Brenda Dickinson and B R Hartley.

The catalogue of plain samian is on microfiche 10–13.

Summary

The site produced large quantities of samian, generally in a good state of preservation, with only a few abraded sherds. There were 32 stamps and 166 decorated sherds, though many of the latter were extremely small. The most significant feature was the small number of South Gaulish pieces and the corresponding preponderance of Central Gaulish wares (see graph, fig 19).

South Gaul	26 sherds	15.5%
Central Gaul	135 sherds	81.5%
East Gaul	5 sherds	3.0%

Most of the South Gaulish vessels were Flavian with only a few sherds, either decorated or plain, of pre-Flavian date. The majority of the 2nd century samian consisted of Lezoux products of Hadrianic to early Antonine date. Such a concentration of Central Gaulish wares is surprising, as sites in the London area usually produce up to 60% South Gaulish vessels, and this probably indicates intensive occupation on the site during the 2nd century. That this pattern may not be typical of Staines as a whole is shown by figures from the nearby Barclays Bank site (report unpublished; information from W J Rodwell) where there was a far higher proportion of South Gaulish samian (approximately 2:3). The flood deposit (Phase XI) which covered the site was unusual as it contained no samian after *c* AD 180, but sealed a pit (59) containing a coin of Caracalla and early 3rd century Rhineland wares. This suggests a period in the late 2nd century of a relatively low level of occupation, resulting in few very late 2nd or early 3rd century pieces becoming incorporated in the flood deposit

The samian stamps

BRENDA DICKINSON and B R HARTLEY

1. ⟨ALBIN⟩ ALBIN[VS], form 33, Albinus ii, die 8b, Lezoux;[1] Phase XI (10).

   The stamp appears on forms 18/31, 18/31R, 27, 31 and 33, and has been recorded from Chesterholm. Other stamps of his are known from Binchester, Castlecary, Halton Chesters and in a group of burnt samian of mid-late Antonine date from Gauting. *c* AD 150–180.

2. ⟨BIAII⟩ BIAI[BINIM], form 18/31, Balbinus, die 2a, Les Martres-de-Veyre;[1] Phase XVI (8).

   This is from a die that deteriorated with use, but originally gave BALBINIM. There are seven examples in the Second London Fire deposit. Balbinus was one of the Trajanic–Hadrianic potters of Les Martres, working *c* AD 100–125.

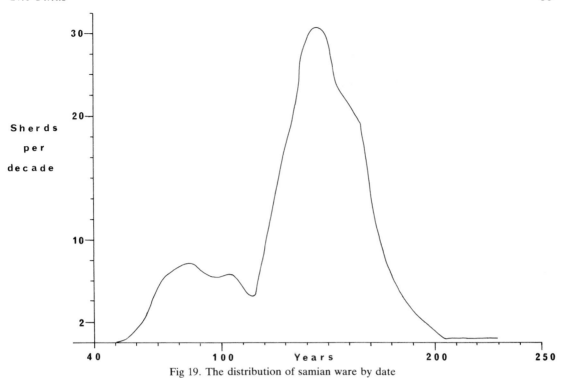

Fig 19. The distribution of samian ware by date

3. 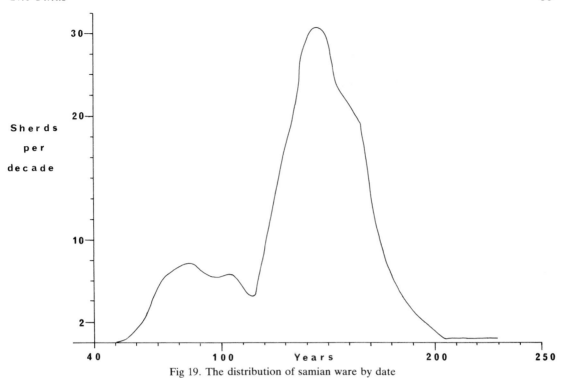 OF[BASSI·CO], form 15/17 or 18, Bassus i-Coelus, die 5b, La Graufesenque;[1] Phase VII/VIII (14).

This stamp was used mainly on rouletted dishes, but occasionally on form 29, with decoration typical of the period *c* AD 55–70. Burnt.

4. BRICC///F, form 27, Briccus, die 7a, Lezoux;[3] Phase XI (10).

This stamp is known from Mumrills and others of his appear frequently on form 38, and occasionally on forms 44 and 80. Slightly burnt. *c* AD 150–180.

5. BVCCVF, form 33, Buccus, die 2c, La Madeleine;[2] Phase IX (35).

While there is no particular dating evidence for this stamp, which appears on forms 18/31R, 31 and 33, Buccus' general record shows him to have been a Hadrianic–Antonine potter, making forms 18/31 and 27 and, very occasionally, an early version of form 32. *c* AD 130–160.

6. COCC[IL.M], form 18/31R, Coccillus, die 5a, Banassac,[1] Lezoux,[1] Vichy (Terre-Franche);[1] Phase VII/VIII (14).

The sequence of migration is not certain, but much of Coccillus' output seems to be from Banassac. However, since Banassac ware is rare in Britain this vessel is more likely to be from Lezoux, or less probably, Vichy. The stamp can best be dated by its presence in a group from a grave at Riempst together with stamps of Cerialis ii, Iulianus i-Tem., Illiomarus ii, Nigrinus ii, and Paullus iv (*Bull Inst Archéol Liégeois*, **67** (1949–50), 41). *c* AD 140–170.

7. (CRAG ·Đ) CRACVNA.F, form 18/31, Cracuna i, die 2a, Lezoux;[1] Phase IX (30). (30).

The stamp is dated by its presence at Verulamium (Period IIB) and in groups of early–mid-Antonine samian from Alcester and the Castleford pottery shop, and at Castlecary. It was used mainly on forms 18/31 and 27. Base deliberately chipped. *c* AD 130–160.

8. VICATVS [DI]VICATUS, form 33, Divicatus, die 3a, Lezoux;[1] Phase XI (10).

There are numerous examples of the stamp from the Castleford pottery shop of AD 140–150, and it appears on forms 27, 31R, 44, 80 and Ludowici Tg. *c* AD 140–170.

9. (FIRM) FIRMV[SF.C], form 33, Firmus ii, die 5a, Rheinzabern,[1] Heiligenberg,[2] Ittenweiler;[2] Phase XI (9).

Firmus' output came mainly from Rheinzabern, where his forms include 31R, 32, and 40 and decorated ware of the late 2nd century. One of his stamps is known from Newstead. As the examples at Heiligenberg and Ittenweiler are on plain ware it is likely that he worked briefly at one, or both, of these factories. *c* AD 160–200.

10. (M·F) M.F.[GEMINI.M], form 45, Geminus vi, die 1a, Lezoux;[2] unstratified.

As this stamp is known only on form 45, which was not introduced at Lezoux before AD 170, a date *c* AD170–200 is certain.

11. (C) H[ABILISM], form 31, Habilis, die 1a, Lezoux;[1] Phase XII (28).

There are many examples of this stamp at Lezoux on forms including 27, 38 and 80. Habilis' work appears in mid-late Antonine contexts there, and as he occasionally made form 27, a date *c* AD 150–180 is likely. Burnt.

12. (IOENALISF) IOENALISF, form 33, Ioenalis i, die 1a, Les Martres-de-Veyre;[1] Phase XI (10).

There are five examples of this stamp in the Second London Fire deposit, and it appears on form 37 with Trajanic decoration (impressed, after moulding, under the base). Slightly burnt. *c* AD 100–120.

13. (LC LLI·M) LO.LLI.M, form 18/31R, Lollius ii, die 2a, Lezoux;[1] Phase XIII (203).

The stamp appears on a wide range of forms, including 15/31, 18/31, 27, 42, 79, 80 and Ludowici Tg. It occurs at Camelon, Catterick and Hadrian's Wall (Chesters Museum). *c* AD 140–170.

14. (VFEVoSF) LVTEVOSF, form 31, Lutevos, die 2a, Rheinzabern;[1] Phase X (59).

There is virtually no dating evidence for this potter, who may or may not be the same as the Luteus who made decorated ware of the late 2nd–early 3rd century. This stamp occurs at Malton and on form 31R and 31. Another is on the rim of a bowl of form 37, with the ovolo too fragmentary to identify with any of Luteus. A date *c* AD 160–220 should cover the range.

15. (MAC) MAC[RINI], form 31, Macrinus iii, die 5b, Lezoux;[2] Phase XVI (8).

The site record includes Chesters, Newstead and the Wroxeter Gutter (2) and the forms are 31, 33 and one 27, *c* AD 150–180.

16. [MAC]RINI, form 38, Macrinus iii, die 5c, Lezoux;[2] Phase XI (10).

One of Macrinus iii's less common stamps, which has not been noted in a dated context. Probably *c* AD 150–180 on his general record.

17. [MAIVE]ILUSF (the F is not absolutely certain), form 33?, Maiudilus, die 3a, Lezoux;[1] Phase XII (151).

Maiudilus is known only by this stamp, which occurs in the Castleford pottery shop deposit, at Catterick and on forms 18/31, 27 and 33. *c* AD 135–155.

18. [MARCE]LLI.M, form 33?, Marcellus iii, die 2g, Lezoux;[2] Phase VIII (36).

The stamp is in the Period IID fire deposits at Verulamium and on forms 18/31, 18/31R and 33. His other work is known from Hadrian's Wall and Scotland and his forms include 42, 79 and 80. *c* AD 140–170.

19. MATURIM, form 33?, Maturus ii, die 1c, Lezoux;[2] Phase XI (10).

The stamp has been recorded from Alcester (on an early variety of form 31R in a mid-Antonine pit) and on forms 18/31R and 27. As Maturus also made forms 79 and 80, a date *c* AD 145–175 is likely.

20. OV[IDIM], form 18/31, Ovidus?, die 1a, Les-Martres-de-Veyre;[1] Phase IXA (191).

Nearly always on form 27 and occurs several times at Les Martres. Two examples also from the Second London Fire. *c* AD 100–120.

21. –ATERCLO[SFE+], form 18/31, Paterclus ii, die 10a, Les Martres-de-Veyre;[1] Phase VII (56).

The final, and most common, version of a stamp originally giving PATERCLOSFE, it occurs on forms 18/31 and 27, at Malton, Nether Denton and in the Second London Fire deposit. *c* AD 110–125.

22. PATER[ ], form 27, Paternus, Central Gaul; Phase IX (30).

One of the earlier Paterni dating to the early Antonine period. Burnt.

23. [ROP]PVSFE, form 18/31, Roppus ii, die 1a, Les Martres-de-Veyre;[2] Phase XI (10).

As this stamp has been noted twice from Castleford (probably from the group from the pottery shop) and from the Saalburg Erdkastell, a date *c* AD 110–145 is likely. Slightly burnt and riveted.

24. [RV]FFI.MA, form 18/31, Ruffus ii, die 1a, Lezoux;[2] Phase IX (30).

The site record includes Cappuck, the Castleford pottery shop and Newstead, and the forms are 18/31, 18/31R, 27, 31 and 33. *c* AD 140–170.

25. RVFF[I·MA], form 33, Ruffus ii, die 1a, Lezoux;[2] Phase XI (10).

See above, no 24.

26. [T].RVFIN, form 18, (T.) Rufinus ii, die 25a, La Graufensenque;[2] Phase VII/VIII (14).

The record for this stamp seems to be entirely Flavian and the sites include Caerleon and Corbridge. *c* AD 70–90.

27. TARV[I], form 31, Tarvus i, die 1a, East Gaul;[3] Phase XV (5).

The only other certain example of this stamp is from London, the fabric of which, together with the distribution for attributed stamps of this potter, suggests origin in one of the Argonne factories. Antonine.

28. ATIVIIII, form 33, illiterate stamp, Central Gaul; unstratified. Mid–late Antonine.

29.]NI or IN[, form 33, illegible, Central Gaul; Phase XI (143). Antonine.

30. Illegible on form 18/31, East Gaul?, La Madeleine?; unstratified.

Hadrianic–Antonine.

31.]EM[, illegible, dish with kick; Phase IXA (53).

The fabric and triple grooving are unusual. This could be 1st century Lezoux ware or from one of the East Gaulish factories, and is therefore not datable.

32. ANTONIANI·M form 33, Antonianus, die 1a, Les Martres-de-Veyre; unstratified (1970 excavation by Mrs M Rendell).

Only example in Britain. Date uncertain, *c* AD 100–170. This stamp was among the material examined by Dr W J Rodwell.

Notes

[1] Stamps from the same die are attested at the pottery or potteries in question.
[2] Stamps from other dies of the potter known there.
[3] Assigned to a pottery or potteries on distribution and/or fabric.

Decorated samian

Some residual decorated samian has been omitted from the following catalogue. Context numbers are given in parentheses after the description, except for Phase VII/VIII where only one context was recorded.

Abbreviations

S, C, EG:	South, Central, East Gaul
O:	figure-types from Oswald 1936–7
Rogers:	types from Rogers 1974
S & S:	Stanfield & Simpson 1958

fig 20

Phase VIA

1. Dr 37, CG. Style of X-2 of Les Martres-de-Veyre. His ovolo without typical border (S & S pl 5, no 52). Below is a tendril and gladiator, as Terrisse 1968, pl 25, no 10010. *c* AD 100–120. (Probably intrusive, found in top 20mm of 176) (Illustrated)

Phase VII

2. Dr 37, CG. Tendril with bifid leaf? Hadrianic–early Antonine. (56)
3. Dr 37, CG. Superbly executed bowl with silky slip of Quintilianus. His ovolo 1 above wavy line border; beneath, the bowl is divided into panels. The chariot is O.101 variant and both the ornaments were used by him (Rogers L 12 and U 28). *c* AD 125–150. Some sherds slightly burnt. (56) (Illustrated)
4. Dr 37, CG. Double-bordered ovolo with beaded tongue ending in a rosette, perhaps Rogers B 16 used by Sacer–Attianus. The fragment of vertical wavy line suggests the latter. *c* AD 130–150. (56)

Phase VII/VIII (14)

5. Dr 37, CG. Style of Divixtus. His ovolo 2 with beaded border and small double medallion containing a ring (S & S pl 116, no 8, *etc*). *c* AD 150–180. (Illustrated)
6. Dr 37, EG. Style of Saturninus/Satto (see also no 100 below). The general scheme is similar to the other bowl, but has a different leaf (Lutz 1970, V 23) and the overlapping ovolo is Lutz O 1. Early–mid C2. (Illustrated)
7. Dr 37, CG. Satyr (O.590) and nude woman (S & S pl 48, no 576). Both were used by 'Donnaucus' (X-13), but the border ending in a seven-beaded rosette is suggestive of the Donnaucus–Sacer group (S & S pl 84, no 2). *c* AD 110–130. (Illustrated)
8. Dr 37, CG. Style of X-6. Typical border with Bacchus (O.571) and ornament (Rogers Q 89) (S & S pl 74, nos 5, 11). Slightly burnt. *c* AD 130–150. (Illustrated)
9. Dr 37, CG. Nude man (O.688) used by several potters. The hand has been obscured by a brush-like motif. Hadrianic–early Antonine. (Illustrated)
10. Dr 37, SG. Fragment of extremely large leaf. Flavian.
11. Dr 37, SG. Festoon with cordate stipuled bud in toothed demi-medallion, used by Passenus (Karnitsch 1959, taf 8, no 4). Burnt. *c* AD 70–90.
12. Dr 29, SG. Bush motif used by several late potters, but also earlier on this form by Pudentius (Knorr 1919, taf 68). *c* AD 65–80.
13. Dr 37, CG. The rider (O.245) was used by several potters, but the use of the acanthus leaf fillers suggests the work of Criciro. *c* AD 135–175.
14. Dr 37, CG. Blurred ovolo 1 of Attianus. *c* AD 130–150.
15. Dr 37, CG. Double-bordered ovolo with beaded rosette tongue; probably a leaf beneath. Burnt. Hadrianic–early Antonine.

16. Dr 37, CG. Demi-medallion with rabbit (similar to O.2116), used by several potters. Slightly burnt. Hadrianic–early Antonine.
17. Dr 37, CG. Blurred rosette, possibly of Drusus II. *c* AD 125–145.
18. Dr 37, CG. Large bowl, of which the whole design, panels divided by wavy lines, survives. The figures are a dancer (O.345) in a double medallion, Osiris (O.711a; Hartley, B R, 1972, fig 95, no 94), a leaf (Rogers J 89) and Minerva (O.126). There is no upper border and the large ovolo seems to be Cinnamus ovolo 4. However, the style of the bowl is not his, nor does it apparently fit into that of any other well known potter. General design, borders, circles, *etc*, and the fabric, suggest a date *c* AD 130–160. One sherd burnt. (Illustrated)
19. Dr 37, CG. Cinnamus ovolo 3a above panel decoration of nude man (O.687) in demi-medallion and small double medallion containing uncertain figure type. The design has some links with the work of Doeccus. Very orange fabric. *c* AD 150–180.

Phase VIII

20. Dr 37, CG. Finely executed piece with silky slip typical of Quintilianus. His ovolo (Rogers B 28) with fine wavy line borders and small double circle. The vine scroll is Rogers M 5, used by him (S & S pl 69, no 14 has a similar scheme). *c* AD 125–145. (Illustrated)
21. Dr 37, CG. Victory (O.812) in a double medallion with fragment of astragalus in the corner. Similar designs were frequently used by Laxtucissa (Karnitsch 1959, taf 43, nos 1–4). *c* AD 150–180. (36) (Illustrated)
22. Dr 37, CG. Presumably by a Hadrianic–early Antonine potter, although it is not clear which, and unfortunately the ovolo, which has a blurred rosette terminal, is too fragmentary for identification. The wreath recalls the work of Avitus and Vegetus, although this is closest to Rogers G 306 used by P-3. The gladiator was used by the Quintilianus group and X-6/Large-S potter. Burnt. Thick fabric. *c* AD 125–150. (40) (Illustrated)
23. Dr 37, CG. The triton (O.25 variant) was used by Libertus and both he and his associate Butrio used the coarse roped border. The terminal of rosette and leaf is perhaps that shown on S & S fig 13, no 5 and on Karnitsch 1959, taf 33, no 2, used by Butrio. The figure above is uncertain but might be a mask. Very thin fabric. *c* AD 120–145. (44) (Illustrated)
24. Dr 37, CG. An interesting piece with winding scroll and tendrils ending in a small leaf, which might be Rogers H 131, beneath a blurred border. The field contains small circles and the Cerialis–Cinnamus leaf tip. The general design is similar to a bowl by Tittius and Cassia (S & S pl 146, no 2), which has the small leaf. A Tittius, possibly same potter, was a bowl finisher of Cinnamus (S & S 271). *c* AD 130–160. (36) (Illustrated)
26. Dr 37, CG. Style of X-6. His ovolo (S & S fig 18, no 2) above wavy line border and winding scroll design. The individual motifs are a vine scroll

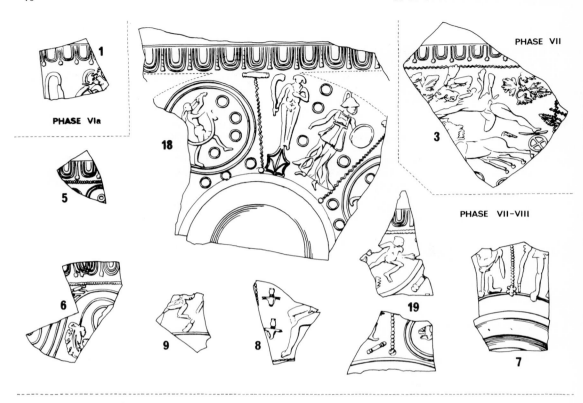

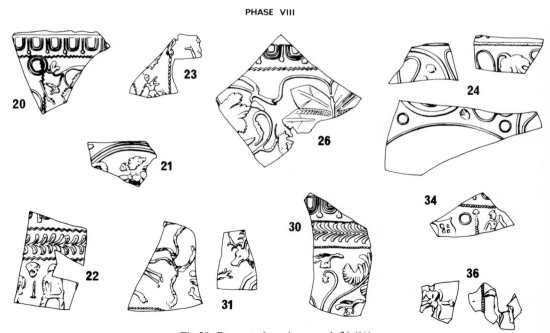

Fig 20. Decorated samian, nos 1–36 (½)

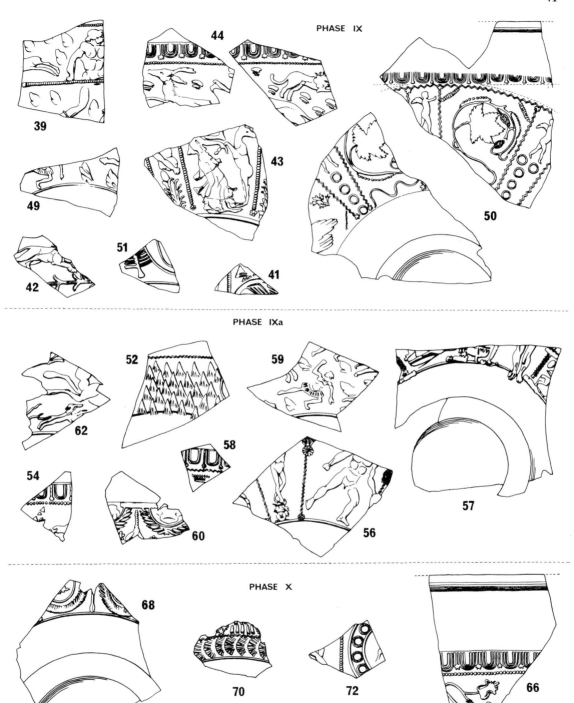

Fig 21. Decorated samian, nos 39–72 (½)

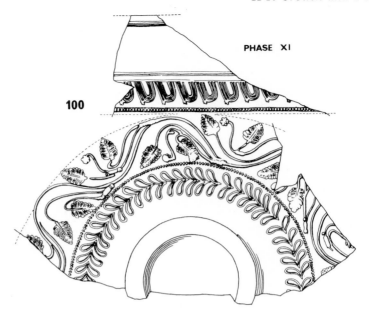

PHASE XI

100

Fig 22. Decorated samian, no 100 (½)

(Rogers M 8), a bunch of grapes and a large leaf (Rogers H 43; *cf* S & S pl 75, no 22). The leaf occurs on a Martres sherd from Little Chester (Hartley 1971, fig 4, no 34), and at Tongres (Schaetzen & Vanderhoeven 1953–4, pl 34, no 11) on a bowl probably with X-6's ovolo 4. The piece clearly shows turning marks from the interior of the mould. *c* AD 130–150. (36) (Illustrated)

27. Dr 37, CG. Diagonal, square-beaded border. Burnt. Hadrianic–early Antonine. (36)

28. Dr 37, CG. Fragment of scroll design similar to those used by Sacer and Cinnamus. *c* AD 130–170. (36)

29. Dr 37, CG. Back legs and tail of dog (probably O.1917), used by Libertus and several other Lezoux potters. Hadrianic–early Antonine. (44).

30. Dr 37, SG. The leaf (Hartley, B R, 1972, fig 94, no 80) is attributed by Karnitsch (1959, taf 2, no 8) to Calvus, who also used the ovolo (Knorr 1919, taf 16, no 13) and perhaps the bird (*ibid* taf 17, no 33). *c* AD 70–90. (44) (Illustrated)

31. Dr 37, CG. Style of 'Donnaucus' (X-13) of Martres. The stylised tree is more typical of the Potter of the Rosette, but the base is exactly paralleled on S & S pl 47, no 555. The small leaf tips are attached by astragali. To the right is a deer (O.1768) used by 'Donnaucus', and the rear legs of another to the left. Below is a fragment of the basal wreath with fine beaded borders (S & S pl 47, no 549). *c* AD 100–125. (44) (Illustrated)

32. Dr 37, CG. Fragment of double bordered ovolo. Early–mid-C2. (52)

33. Dr 37, CG. Fragment of ovolo. Hadrianic–mid-Antonine. (54)

34. Dr 37, CG. Style of Cinnamus group. Panel decoration divided by astragalus borders. Figures are a small warrior (O.1059) and the lyre of seated Apollo (O.83). Both were used by Cinnamus (S & S pl 159, no 27; pl 160, no 41) and also by his associate Anunus II (Simpson & Rogers 1969, fig 4, nos 27, 28). *c* AD 150–170. (54) (Illustrated)

35. Dr 37, CG. Cinnamus ovolo 3a above beaded border. *c* AD 150–170. (54)

36. Dr 37, CG. Style of the Potter of the Rosette, of Les Martres. The Pan (O.723) is shown on S & S pl 20, no 254, and the beadrows are typical of his work. The cupid (O.395) was used by X-2. Burnt. *c* AD 100–120. (142) (Illustrated)

37. Dr 37, CG. Cigar twist and unidentifiable decoration. Early–mid-Antonine. (149)

Phase IX

39. Dr 37, CG. Part of freestyle design showing a hunter carrying an astragalus-beaded spear, with legs of ? deer to the left. Both Attianus and Criciro used a similar figure (identified in S & S 211, as O.684a), but this is slightly different having boots and is almost certainly a smith (O.65) without his tools. Moreover, neither potter used astragalus borders. A close parallel is given by an unattributed sherd from Tongres (Schaetzen & Vanderhoeven 1953–4, pl 41, no 9) which has similar fillers and a booted hunter. The Tongres sherd

might be attributed to the Cinnamus group, who used astragalus borders and O.65. *c* AD 140–170. (30) (Illustrated)

41. Dr 37, CG. Bird (O.2250a) above ornament (Rogers T 38?) to the left of an astragalus border, both used by Albucius. *c* AD 150–180. (30) (Illustrated)
42. Dr 37, CG. Lion (O.1404 variant) over basal wreath of trifid leaves. The very high quality slip and basal wreath suggest the work of the Quintilianus group (S & S pl 68, nos 3, 8; pl 70, no 17). *c* AD 125–150. (30) (Illustrated)
43. Dr 37, CG. Panel decoration of alternating caryatids (O.1207 variant) and Diana with dog? (O.106) divided by medium-fine borders ending in a small rosette. S & S pl 112, no 8, and pl 115, nos 1, 2, show very similar bowls by Divixtus and Advocisus, but also see Karnitsch 1959, taf 65, no 1, for this design used by Cinnamus. *c* AD 150–180. (30) (Illustrated)
44. Dr 37, CG. Style of Sacer–Attianus. Free-style design with lion (O.1404), deer (O.1781?) and leopard (O.1537) (S & S pl 86, nos 12, 15). The leaf tips (S & S pl 85, no 9) suggest the work of the latter potter. *c* AD 130–150. (30) (Illustrated)
48. Dr 37, CG. The leaf tip suggests Cerialis–Cinnamus style and Karnitsch (1959, taf 70, no 2) shows a similar design with a winding scroll. *c* AD 140–160. (133) (Illustrated)
49. Dr 37, CG. Free style design with warrior (O.177) and leaf tips. Very similar to no 59 below, and the same comments apply, except that this piece is considerably thicker with a matt slip. *c* AD 140–170. (183) (Illustrated)
50. Dr 37, CG. Panel decorated bowl with wavy line borders. The panels contain a vine scroll (Rogers M 2), cupid (O.404, with arm broken?), circles and an eagle (O.2162 variant, used by Mercator I: S & S fig 51, no 1) with a small leaf and a decorative detail. Although the ovolo is Casurius' no 4 the general style is that of Tetturo (S & S pl 131, nos 1, 2), who used similar terminals. Burnt. Early–mid Antonine. (236) (Illustrated)
51. Dr 37, CG. Fragment of winding scroll with small leaf beneath (probably Rogers J 131) only recorded on the work of Laxtucissa, although the fabric of this piece suggests a slightly earlier date. Mid C2. (236) (Illustrated)

Phase IXA

52. Dr 37, CG. Panel of arrowheads below fine wavy line. The fabric indicates this piece comes from Martres. Burnt. *c* AD 100–125. (53) (Illustrated)
54. Dr 37, CG. Ovolo (Rogers B 12) used by several Lezoux potters, notably Sacer, Criciro and Divixtus. Below a beaded border is a partly impressed leaf. Mid C2. (53) (Illustrated)
56. Dr 37, CG. Very finely moulded panel decorated bowl divided by wavy lines ending in an 8-pointed rosette and a 12-pointed rosette with bifid leaf above (?Rogers C 236—Birrantus, *etc*). The fi-

gures are a winged cupid, used by Laxtucissa (S & S pl 99, no 16), and Bacchus (O.578) used by Censorinus. However, the general character of the bowl suggests an earlier date, so perhaps the work of the Quintilianus group. *c* AD 130–150. (53) (Illustrated)

57. Dr 37, CG. Base of panel decorated bowl with vertical beaded borders and astragalus terminals. The identifiable figures are a seated Apollo (O.84) and nude man (O.637). Both were used by Attianus but he used simple rosette terminals. The astragali recall the work of Docilis/Doccalus (S & S pl 93, no 17, *etc*) and of Cettus (S & S pl 142, nos 27, 33), who also used the figures. *c* AD 130–160. (53) (Illustrated)
58. Dr 37, CG. Style of X-2 of Les Martres-de-Veyre. His ovolo above wavy line and typical ornament (S & S pl 3, no 3). *c* AD 100–120. (53) (Illustrated)
59. Dr 37, CG. Style of Cinnamus group. Freestyle design with warrior (O.177; Karnitsch 1959, taf 70, no 1) and legs of animals. Several associates of Cinnamus used the warrior and this piece might be by one of them, perhaps Paullus (*cf* S & S pl 165, no 3). *c* AD 140–160. (53) (Illustrated)
60. Dr 37, CG. The ovolo seems to have been completely removed during the finishing process. Festoon arrangement of demi-medallions (Rogers F 19) containing smudged details, perhaps masks. The beaded swag ends in a trifid leaf flanked by a 7-beaded rosette. The general design is not dissimilar to some Martres work, especially by the Potter of the Rosette (S & S pl 20, no 250). However, the fabric indicates that this is a Lezoux piece, so presumably *c* AD 120–150. Burnt. (53) (Illustrated)
62. Dr 37, CG. Free-style design with dog (O.1926a) and deer (O.1805), both used by Butrio (S & S pl 57, no 653; pl 59, no 667). *c* AD 120–145. (191) (Illustrated)

Phase X

66. Dr 37, CG. Scroll design, probably by Sacer. The ovolo seems to be his no 4, and he used a similar cigar twist (S & S pl 83, nos 11, 12). The leaf is not exactly paralleled in Rogers, but closest to G 147. *c* AD 125–150. (59) (Illustrated)
68. Dr 37, CG. Simple basal wreath. The rather untidy work is suggestive of X-6 (S & S pl 75, no 15). *c* AD 130–150 (141) (Illustrated)
70. Dr 37, SG. Wavy line borders with rosette terminals. Small panel of arrowheads above basal wreath. Flavian. (173) (illustrated)
71. Dr 37, SG. For similar festoon designs, see Knorr 1952, taf 37, A, attributed to Biragillus. *c* AD 75–95. (174) (Illustrated)
72. Dr 37, CG. Style of Aventinus II. The double medallion with small corded circles is shown on S & S pl 156, nos 7, 8. To the left of an astragalus border are knees of an Apollo (O.83 variant) also used by him (S & S pl 156, no 6). *c* AD 160–190. (174) (Illustrated)

Phase XI

100. Dr 37, EG. Large part of a bowl in the style of Saturninus/Satto, who worked at a number of kiln sites including Boucheporn, Chémery–Faulquemont, Blickweiler and Mittelbronn. The design consists of a winding scroll divided from the ovolo and basal wreath by beaded borders. The individual motifs (after Lutz 1970) are: ovolo O2, border G 2, astragalus G 5, rosette G 12?, leaf V 5 and wreath V 18. Similar schemes are shown in Lutz (1970) and also Fölzer (1913, tafn 3–6).

Products of these potters are rare in Britain: Lutz lists nine sites including London and Silchester, and another piece occurs at Verulamium (Hartley, B R, 1972, fig 98, no 132). Mr Hartley has also informed me that he has seen some two dozen other sherds from sites including Hadrian's Wall and the Pennine forts. It is interesting that there is a second piece from this site (no 6 above) and that another has been found in recent excavations at Brentford (report in preparation). Early-mid C2. (10) (Illustrated)

The other Roman pottery

K R CROUCH and S A SHANKS
figs 23–36

This report was completed by 1979, and therefore does not take account of subsequent research.

We would like to thank the following for their assistance in producing this report: Mrs K F Hartley, for identifying the mortaria; Mrs A Anderson, for her work on the colour-coated pottery; Miss O S Farrington, for her work on the flagons and amphorae; Mr M Lyne, for help in identifying the Alice Holt/Farnham material; Mr C M Green, for assistance with the amphorae; and Mr P Arthur, for his work on the lead glazed pottery.

For the catalogue of illustrated pottery see microfiche 14–34.

Since the material from the Friends' Burial Ground site was in a well stratified sequence, it was decided that to seek many parallels from other sites in the south-east would provide relatively little additional dating information. Instead, the pottery has been arranged by fabric and then by form, following the suggestions of Peacock (1977a). In this way the material can be related where possible to known production sites, and it is hoped that this will enable some new conclusions to be drawn concerning trade between Staines and the various potteries.

From more than 3000 rim sherds recovered from the site, we have selected for illustration only those which provide new information for each phase, *ie*:

(i)   the initial sherds from a new kiln area trading with the town;
(ii) sherds which show changes or expansion in the repertoire or forms within a kiln group;
(iii) sherds of intrinsic interest, which may occur residually.

A full catalogue of all forms within their fabric ranges has been compiled for the archive and is available for inspection by prior arrangement, together with introductory notes on the pottery and analysis system.

The usual abbreviations BB1 and BB2 have been used for the black-burnished wares, which are discussed below under the relevant fabrics.

The pottery fabrics

A. STAINES
     Figs 23–5, 27–31.
     Nos 4, 6, 24, 27–8, 30–1, 61, 77–8, 120–2, 155–6, 176–7, 186, 188, 203?, 208, 227?, 273.

Colour
     Core and margin oxidised orange/red or reduced mid-grey, surfaces orange or grey.

Paste
     Hard, slightly granular fabric, with a smooth fracture.

Inclusions
     Frequent well-sorted sand, less than 0.1mm; frequent well-sorted quartz, less than 0.5mm; moderate well-sorted mica, less than 0.1mm; moderate ill-sorted grog, less than 0.5mm; moderate well-sorted ironstone, 0.1–0.2mm.

Surface treatment
     Mica dusting on beakers and bowls; thin pale orange wash and burnishing on small beakers; thick cream slip on flagons.

The fabric occurs in large amounts in the town, in both oxidised and reduced forms. It comes from the earliest levels on the Quakers' site and on the Central Area Development Site (report in preparation). A kiln producing reduced wares in this fabric was located by Mrs M Rendell on a site just north of the High Street (material with Staines Achaeological Unit)

B. COLNE VALLEY SOUTH (INCLUDING FULMER/HEDGERLEY)

Figs 23–7.
Nos 1–2, 5, 10, 15, 21, 34–8, 45, 62–3, 70, 74–5, 82–95, 135–7.

Colour
Core and margin grey or grey/brown, surfaces sometimes with oxidised orange patches.

Paste
Hard, smooth sandy fabric with a rough fracture.

Inclusions
Abundant well-sorted sub-angular sand, less than 0.1mm;
abundant ill-sorted sub-angular quartz, from 0.2–1.2mm;
moderate ill-sorted irregular grog particles, up to 1.0mm;
moderate well-sorted round black ironstone, approx 0.2mm;
moderate well-sorted mica, approx 0.1mm.

Surface treatment
Sometimes irregular burnishing, or a surface wipe; decoration is generally restricted to grooves or cordons, and occasionally a series of stabbed lines (nos 94–95), glazing, and mica-dusting.

The products of this industry first appear in Phase V *c* AD 60, with 'Surrey' bowls and bead rim jars. These forms are not present amongst the published pottery from either the Fulmer (Corder 1943) or Hedgerley (Oakley *et al* 1937) kilns, but are of such similar fabric that the clay source and method of manufacture must be allied. The kilns at Fulmer and Hedgerley have been dated to the early–mid-2nd century, and their forms include imitation BB1 pie dishes (Corder 1943, fig 7, no 3) and shouldered jars (*ibid*, no 8), but the absence of the 'Surrey' bowl form must point to the discontinuation of this bowl form from the repertoire of these potters by the early 2nd century in favour of the pie dish and reeded-rim bowl. It is likely that the industry was set up in the mid–late 1st century to supply *Pontes* and the surrounding area, and over the course of the next century gradually migrated northwards along the Colne Valley, seeking out new clay and wood sources. The decline of the industry in the late 2nd century coincides with the general decline of the town.

One of the earliest forms so far recognised in this distinctive fabric is the 'Surrey/Atrebatic' bowl (*eg* fig 23, no 2). These bowls, with girth cordons and grooved rims, are widely distributed throughout most of Surrey and parts of Hampshire and Berkshire. Examples of these bowls are found at Brentford (Canham 1978a, 53) and Southwark (Marsh & Tyers 1978, 577, type IV K) from early Roman contexts. They also occur in large numbers in Period I at Silchester (Cotton 1947, 153), and at Fishbourne (Cunliffe 1971, 220, type 208, wrongly reconstructed with a footring), where they are dated before AD 75. At Chichester (Down 1974, 125) they were found in conquest levels, and recent excavations at the possible Neronian fort site at Wanborough have produced examples (Anderson & Wacher 1980, fig 5, no 8). Other sites with published parallels are Winchester (Cunliffe 1964, 64–5 and fig 17, no 283), Purberry Shot (Lowther 1949, 42) and the cemetery site at Haslemere (Holmes 1949, type 22), where it is described as a typical Surrey form of the Claudian to early Flavian period.

Fifty-seven vessels in this form were found on the Friends' Burial Ground site, and although this number is large compared to other sites in south-east England, other sites in Staines usually produce a far higher proportion. The bowls first appear on the site in features dated *c* AD 60 and continue to occur throughout the life of the site, their greatest concentration being in Phases VI–VII (*c* AD 60–130). On the Central Area Development site (report in preparation) they appear in very large numbers in pre-AD 60 contexts, and therefore it seems that these bowls should be regarded as a pre-Flavian development of a native form.

It is more difficult to fix a terminal date for this type, but by *c* AD 100 new kiln products were coming into the town (*eg* Verulamium region wares, fabric H), in such large numbers that it would seem reasonable to suggest that they were either filling a void left by a waning industry or

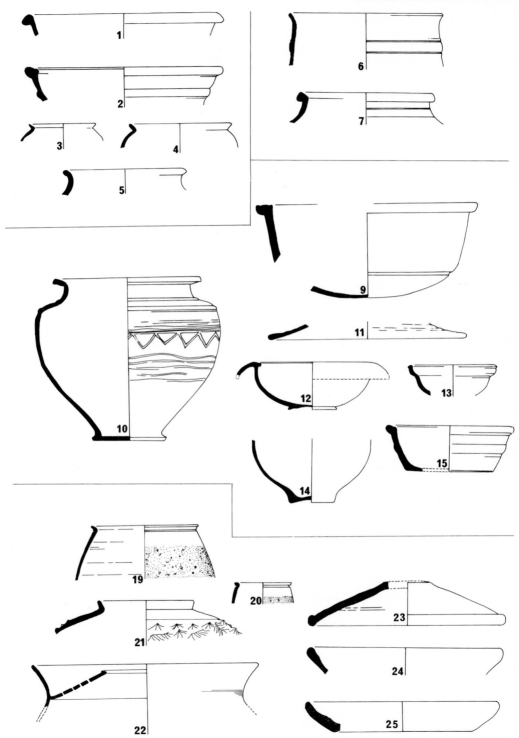

Fig 23. Roman pottery, nos 1–25 (¼)

flooding the town with factory-produced wares to obtain the market. It is probable that *c* AD 100 the Colne Valley potters moved further northward to the Hedgerley and Fulmer area, and here it is noticeable that this 'Surrey' bowl is absent but that copies of BB1 bowls were being produced, indicating the end of the tradition. It may therefore be suggested that the date range of the 'Surrey/Atrebatic' bowl from the kilns in the Colne Valley is possibly pre-conquest to *c* AD 100.

C. LOWER THAMES VALLEY (INCLUDING HIGHGATE WOOD)

Figs 23–5, 27, 29–30
Nos 3, 11, 32–3, 69, 79–81, 128–30, 134, 174, 197, 200

Colour
Core, margin and surfaces mid-grey, occasionally grey/brown.

Paste
Hard smooth fabric with a finely granular appearance and an irregular fracture.

Inclusions
Frequent well-sorted sub-angular sand, approx 0.1mm;
frequent–moderate well-sorted quartz, 0.1mm;
sparse well-sorted round ironstone, 0.1–0.2mm;
sparse well-sorted mica, approx 0.1mm;
occasional sparse well-sorted grog particles, approx 0.1mm.

Surface treatment
In almost all examples the ware has a thin light grey slip, which is burnished to a silvery finish; some have mica-dusting. 'Poppy' beakers have characteristic panels of barbotine dots, and jars have burnished chevrons on the shoulder.

The fabric of this ware is very similar to kiln wasters from the Highgate Wood kilns (Brown & Sheldon 1970, Group 2, no 7), and the forms are all within the range of the published types of Phase III at that site. These fabrics and forms are found throughout the London area in the late 1st and early 2nd centuries, and it has been suggested that all these vessels are the products of a group of itinerant potters (Marsh & Tyers 1978, 535).

The clays of the Lower Thames Valley are derived from the same geological source and are probably very similar right across the region, so that it is difficult to identify the exact location of manufacture without the presence of a kiln site. It is recognised that the site at Highgate Wood is unlikely to have supplied the wide area from which this ware is recovered, so small-scale localised production of standard forms seems most probable. The unusual 'poppy' beaker forms, nos 32 and 79, are known at Highgate, but not in large numbers (Marsh & Tyers 1978, 569–70), whereas here they represent almost 50% of the 'poppy' beaker forms. In general the everted collared form predominates (no 33).

This ware is present in Staines from Phase VII, *c* AD 80–130, until Phase VIII, *c* AD 130–150, agreeing with the dates given for the Highgate Wood kilns.

D. UNKNOWN LOCATION, PROBABLY LOCAL

Figs 23–5, 29–30.
Nos 25, 29, 65–8, 71–3, 167–8, 182, 196.

Colour
Core, margin and surfaces range from buff through to orange/brown.

Paste
Very fine hard, smooth irregular fracture.

Inclusions
Abundant well-sorted round sand, less than 0.1mm;
moderate well-sorted sub-angular quartz, 0.1mm, clear and white;
sparse–moderate well-sorted angular ironstone, 0.5mm, in black and red;
sparse well-sorted mica, 0.1mm;
very occasionally present are grog, calcite, flint and organic material, ill-sorted, 0.5–1.0mm.

Surface treatment
Mica-dusting and burnishing; occasional decoration of a cordon on bowls otherwise plain; lead glazing.

The products of this source appear in the later part of Phase VII (*c* AD 110/20), reaching a peak *c* AD 150/60, and were still in production *c* AD 200. The principal form is the simple dish (Marsh 1978, type 24), which becomes predominant after *c* AD 150/60.

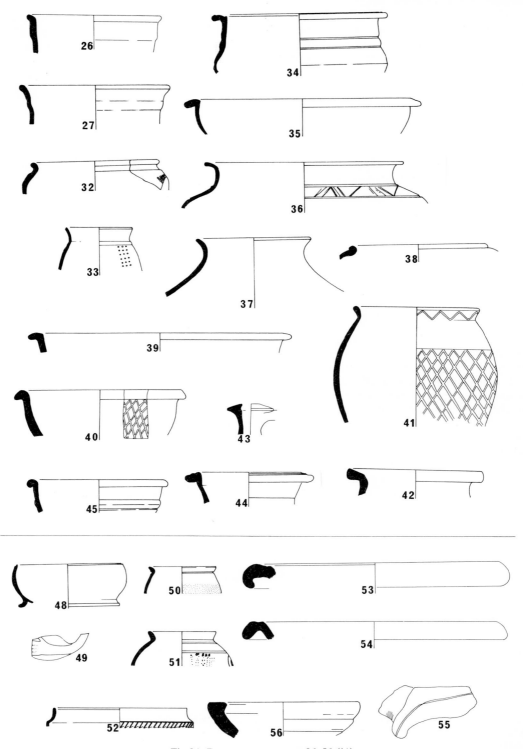

Fig 24. Roman pottery, nos 26–56 (¼)

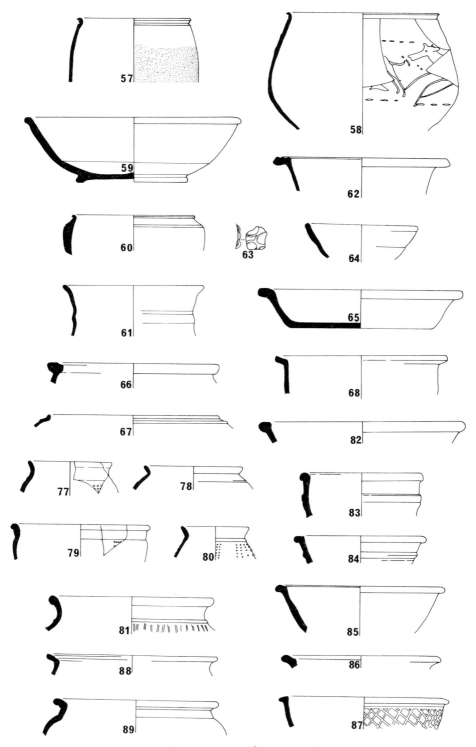

Fig 25. Roman pottery, nos 57–89 (¼)

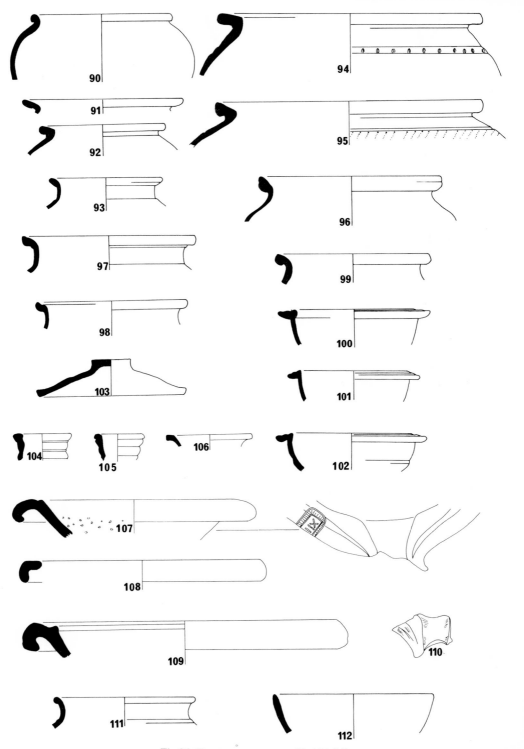

Fig 26. Roman pottery, nos 90–112 (¼)

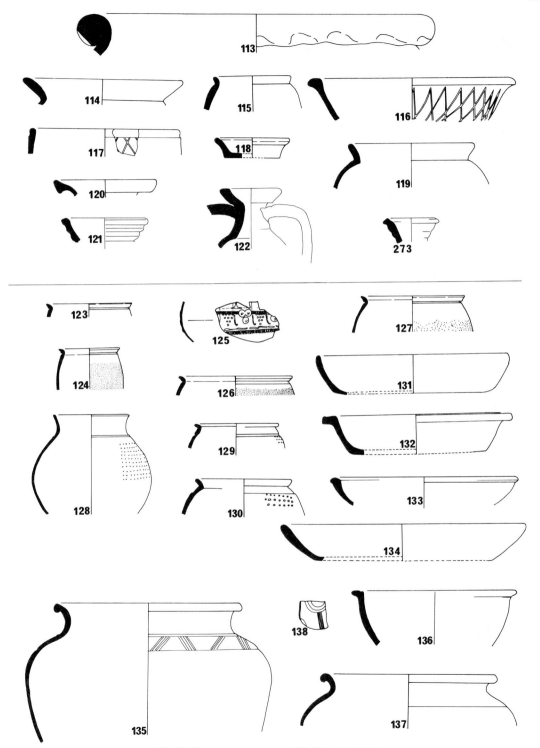

Fig 27. Roman pottery, nos 113–38 and 273 (¼)

E. UNKNOWN LOCATION, PROBABLY LOCAL

Figs 23–5, 27.
Nos 9, 23, 26, 60, 76, 131, 133.

Colour
Pale grey–mid-grey core, orange/brown margins and surfaces.

Paste
Hard, smooth with smooth fracture.

Inclusions
Abundant well-sorted round sand, less than 0.1mm; moderate ill-sorted angular quartz, 0.3–0.5mm, clear, white and grey;
sparse ill-sorted angular ironstone: black 0.2–0.5mm, red 0.5–1.5mm;
sparse well-sorted round grog, yellow/brown, 0.6mm;
sparse well-sorted mica, 0.2mm;
very occasional chalk and organic fragments, 0.5mm or less.

Surface treatment
Burnishing; mica-dusting; occasionally an applied black slip.

The majority of forms are either bowls or dishes. This ware is present in the later part of Phase VII, but only as a very small group, and the major influx comes in Phase IX, *c* AD 150/60–180; the industry ends *c* AD 180/90.

F. UNKNOWN LOCATION

Fig 25.
No 67.

Colour
Mid-grey core, margin and surfaces grey to orange/brown.

Paste
Hard, smooth, irregular granular.

Inclusions
Abundant well-sorted round sand, less than 0.1mm; abundant well-sorted sub-angular quartz, 0.1–0.2mm;
moderate ill-sorted round grog, 1.0mm or less;
moderate well-sorted mica 0.2mm;
moderate well-sorted round ironstone, 0.2mm;
sparse well-sorted shell, 1.5mm.

Surface treatment
Mica dusting, with ridged decoration on shoulder.

The only form present is a beaker. The ware first appears in Phase VIII and lasts up to Phase IX, *c* AD 130–180.

G. UNKNOWN LOCATION

Fig 23.
No 13.

Colour
Core cream/buff, margin and surfaces orange-brown.

Paste
Hard, smooth, smooth irregular fracture.

Inclusions
Abundant well-sorted round sand, less than 0.1mm; moderate well sorted mica, 0.1mm;
moderate ill-sorted round grog, 0.5–1.0mm;
sparse well-sorted sub-angular quartz, 0.2mm;
sparse ill-sorted sub-angular calcite, 0.8mm.

Surface treatment
Burnishing, mica-dusting, and indentation on beakers.

This ware is only found in 1st century contexts, in Phase VIA in a campanulate bowl form and in Phase VII as a sherd from an indented beaker. It may either be from a British kiln site or imported.

H. VERULAMIUM REGION

Figs 23–4, 26, 28–32.
Nos 7–8, 12, 14, 16, 43–4, 46–7, 53–4, 56, 96–110, 139–48, 159–65, 181, 183, 187, 202, 204, 207, 224, 239, 274.

Colour
Core, margin and surfaces off-white through pink and orange to grey/brown, often patchy and irregularly fumed grey. The potters were apparently aiming at a cream/buff.

Paste
Hard and fine with a smooth, sometimes laminar, fracture.

Inclusions
> Frequent well-sorted sub-angular pink, grey and white quartz, approx 0.4–0.5mm;
> moderate irregular orange/red grog, up to 1.0mm;
> occasional sparse well-sorted black ironstone, approx 0.1–0.2mm.

Surface treatment
> All vessels are wheel thrown, and there is no surface treatment beyond an occasional surface wipe. The texture is slightly granular and sandy to the touch. The mortaria have grey and white flints grits on the interior.

The products of several kiln sites in the Verulamium/Brockley Hill area, (*ie* Radlett, Brockley Hill) have been treated as one main group. The earliest kiln site in this production area, Bricket Wood (Saunders & Havercroft 1977), now dated to AD 55, does not seem to have supplied Staines except for the flagon (no 8) in Phase VI and mortarium (no 16) in Phase VIA. Apart from these, the bowl (no 12) from the burial group, in an as yet unparalleled form, is the earliest recovered vessel from the Verulamium region and is dated *c* AD 60. It is of interest that from Phase VII, *c* AD 70–130, a Colne Valley South copy (no 34) of a Verulamium carinated or biconical urn with a reeded rim (Corder 1941, type 6) was recovered, predating any Verulamium region product in this form so far recovered from the town.

The bulk of the Verulamium products do not appear in the town until Phase VIII, *c* AD 130–160, although most of the earlier mortaria originate there. This coincides with the major expansion period of the town, and the new forms include the reeded rim bowls (nos 44 and 100–2) and the shouldered jars (nos 96–7). These forms, although showing many slight variations (Corder 1941, figs 6, 2) remain basically unchanged throughout the period of Staines' trade with the Verulamium region kilns, being thin-walled, with finely formed rims, the bowls having sharply undercut rims and the jars showing a tendency for the rim to turn upwards with sometimes a rebate for a lid (Phases VIII–IX, *c* AD 130–180). Also present in these early phases are examples of Brockley Hill amphorae (no 56).

There appears to be a later revival of this trade with Verulamium, at the time of renewed activity in Staines in Phase XII, *c* AD 260–410. The new forms of this phase, which are not found in features below the Phase XI flooding level and are therefore after *c* AD 220, are obviously of similar origin to those of the earlier phases. The distinctive characteristics of the later vessels are that in both jars and bowls the rims become coarser and larger, and the bodies are thicker, *eg* no 239. There can be little doubt that these variant forms are products of the Verulamium region potteries, as the clay source is identical and the firing and finishing techniques are closely similar. Although no kilns of this late date have yet been excavated in the area, Corder illustrated four typical late jars from Verulamium (Corder 1941, fig 7) which came from 'securely dated deposits' of the late 3rd century and which are close parallels for no 239.

J. FARNHAM/ALICE HOLT

> Figs 24, 26–7, 29, 31–2.
> Nos 42, 111–14, 184, 230–2, 235–7.

Colour
> Core, usually pale grey; margins, often brown/orange; surfaces, mid grey.

Paste
> Hard, smooth fabric with a smooth or laminar fracture.

Inclusions
> Frequent well-sorted sub-angular sand, less than 0.1mm;
> frequent ill-sorted sub-angular quartz, up to 1.0mm;
> moderate well-sorted mica, 0.1mm;
> moderate well-sorted round black ironstone, 0.1–0.2mm;
> occasional irregular grog particles.

Surface treatment
> The most usual surface treatment is an overall silvery burnished slip, particularly on the bowls, and panels of combed lines on the jars.

The Alice Holt/Farnham industry supplied large quantities of pottery to Staines, particularly in the later phases when the local industry in the Colne Valley had ceased production (for full typology and discussion of Alice Holt/Farnham pottery, see Lyne & Jefferies 1979). The earliest

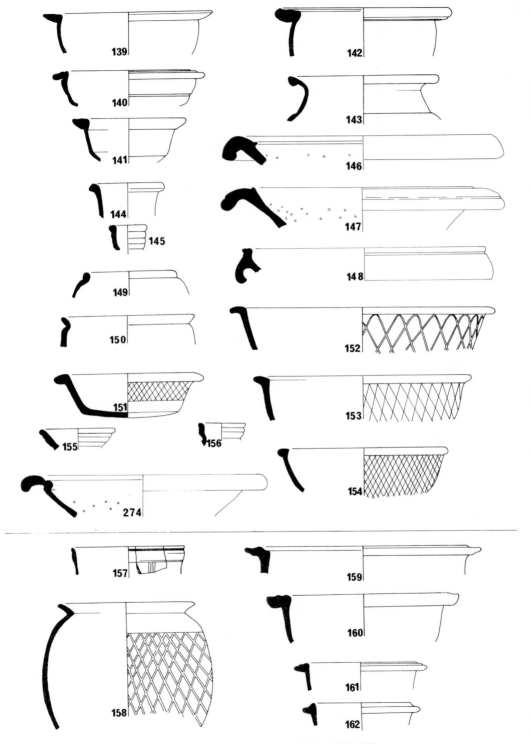

Fig 28. Roman pottery, nos 139–62 and 274 (¼)

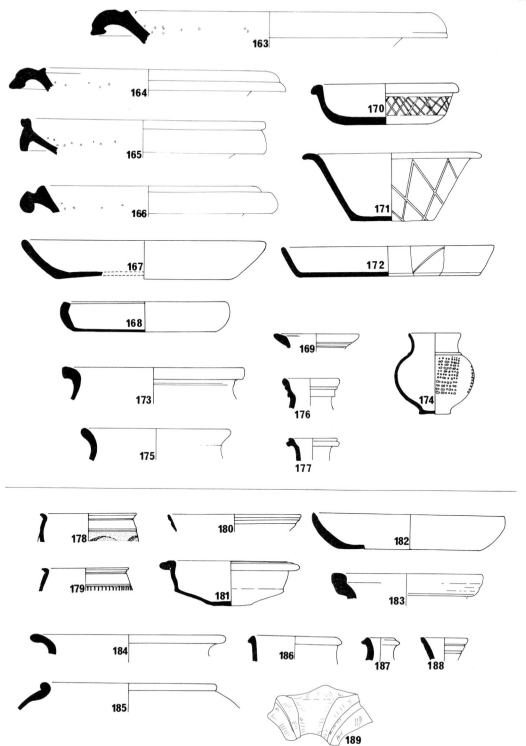

Fig 29. Roman pottery, nos 163–89 (¼)

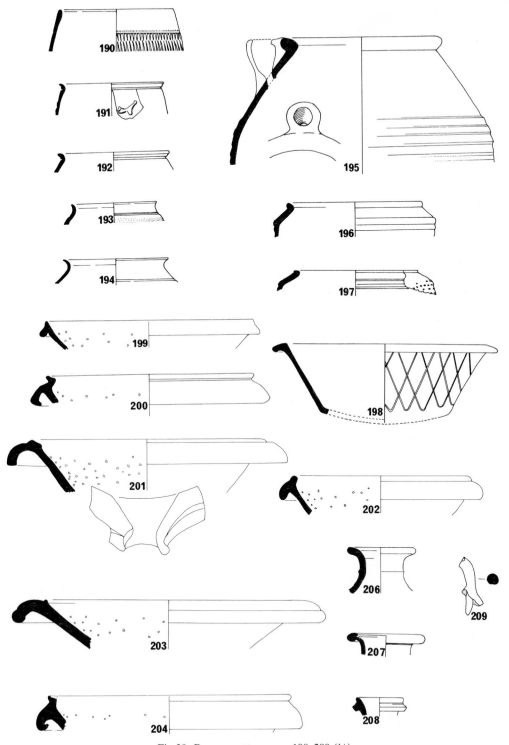

Fig 30. Roman pottery, nos 190–209 (¼)

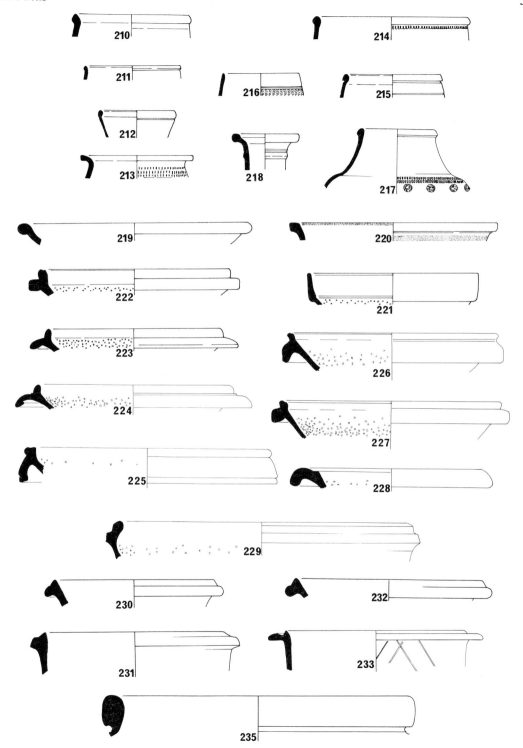

Fig 31. Roman pottery, nos 210–35 (¼)

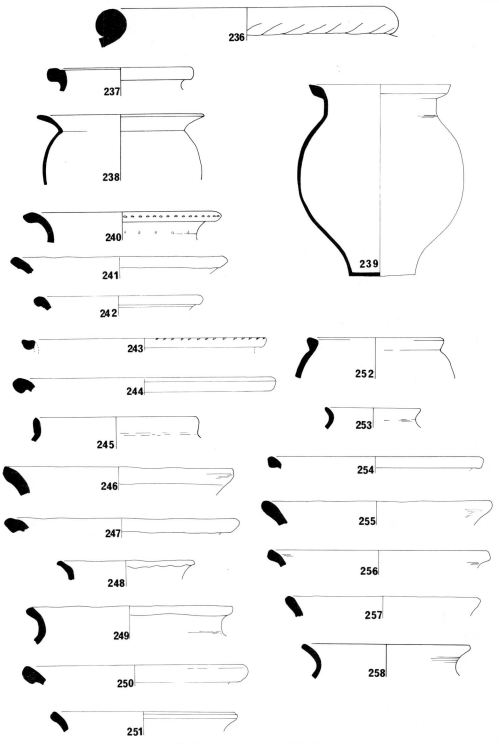

Fig 32. Roman pottery, nos 236–58 (¼)

examples of this ware occur in Phases VII and VIII, it is absent from Phases IX–XI, and reappears in Phase XII, which is the main period for this trade with the introduction of BB1 copies (flanged bowl forms, nos 230–2) and large square-rimmed storage jars (nos 235–7).

K. DORSET/BLACK BURNISHED, BB1

Figs 24, 27–31.
Nos 41, 115–16, 149–52, 170–2, 198, 233.

Colour
Core, margin and surfaces dark brown to black.

Paste
Hard with granular appearance, and an irregular or hackly fracture.

Inclusions
Abundant well-sorted angular white and clear quartz, up to 0.7mm;
moderate well-sorted mica, 0.1mm;
occasional red iron ore in irregular particles, up to 1mm;
occasional irregular limestone fragments, up to 1.00mm;
almost always large irregular particles of shale, up to 4.00mm.

Surface treatment
Hand burnishing overall or in panels, often giving a faceted appearance; charcteristic panels of burnished lattice or looped decoration.

This common ware is a product of the Wareham–Poole Harbour area of Dorset, and is described in detail in several publications (*eg* Farrar 1973; Williams 1977); its origin in Dorset is shown by the presence of shale in the fabric. The ware first appears on this site in Phase VII, *c* AD 80–130, from features dated before *c* AD 120. The most common forms in Staines are the pie dish (nos 116, 151) and the everted rim cooking pot (nos 41, 150). These forms continue unchanged throughout the 2nd century, with the addition *c* AD 150–180 of the incipient flanged bowl form (no 136 in fabric B illustrates the form).

The decline of the town *c* AD 180/90 put a temporary end to this trade which also supplied the town with manufactured items in shale and Purbeck marble, and the resumption of trade in the late 3rd/early 4th centuries is marked by the introduction of a new flanged bowl form (no 233), which only occurs in features above the flooding layer (10), mainly in the black earth deposit (28) dated to the late 3rd–5th centuries. Other BB1 forms include beakers (no 115) and bead rim jars (no 149).

L. UNKNOWN LOCATION (INCLUDES 'LONDON WARE')

Figs 23, 27–29.
Nos 22, 119, 138, 157, 180.

Colour
Core, red/brown; margin, brick red through brown; surfaces, black.

Paste
Hard, smooth fabric with a smooth slightly granular fracture.

Inclusions
Frequent well-sorted sand, less than 0.1mm;
moderate–frequent well-sorted round pellets of grog, up to 0.5mm;
moderate–frequent ill-sorted quartz, up to 0.5mm;
moderate well-sorted ironstone, up to 0.3mm;
sparse–moderate well-sorted mica, 0.1mm;

Surface treament
Thick matt black overall slip, sometimes with incised lines.

This fabric group appears predominantly in small fine beakers and bowls, often decorated with typical 'London ware' inscribed arcs or lines. Two interesting 'incense burners' in this fabric were found on this site (no 22), and a copy of a BB1 jar (no 119). For full discussion, see Marsh 1978.

MI–7. OXFORD REGION

On preliminary analysis of a small selective group of pottery, seven separate fabric groups have been identified from the Oxford kilns. One vessel which had been assigned to Oxford on account of a red/brown colour coat, was found on microscopic analysis to come from the Colne Valley group, fabric B (not illustrated; form as Young 1977, type C45).

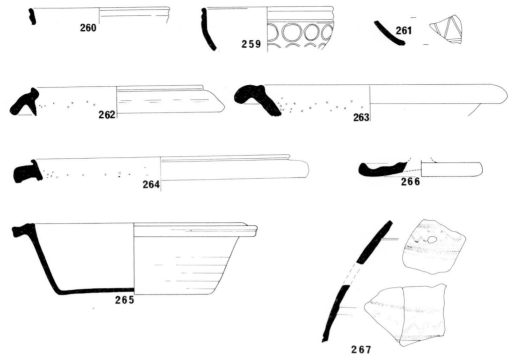

Fig 33. Roman pottery, nos 259–67 (¼)

M1. *White mortaria and 'parchment' wares*

Figs 31, 33.
Nos 215–16, 220, 222, 225–6, 264

Colour
Core, margin and surfaces off-white, occasionally overfired to grey.

Paste
Hard, fine to very slightly granular.

Inclusions
Moderate well-sorted sub-angular quartz, 0.1–0.2mm;

moderate well-sorted round ironstone, 0.2mm – occasionally in the mortaria the ironstone is ill-sorted with frequent angular particles up to 0.5mm; sparse well-sorted mica, 0.1mm.

Surface treatment
The mortaria have no outer surface treatment, the inner having grey, white and pink quartz grits. The 'parchment' wares have a characteristic painted brown/red strip on the rim and body of the pot. All vessels are wheel thrown.

M2. *White mortaria and 'parchment' wares, reduced wares and red/brown colour-coated wares*

Figs 24, 32.
Nos 51, 229.

Colour
Core buff/pink, margin and surfaces cream–off white; reduced wares, core, margin and surfaces grey.

Paste
Hard, very fine fabric.

Inclusions
Generally moderate well-sorted sub-angular quartz,

0.2mm, frequent in mortaria;
moderate ill-sorted sub-angular ironstone, 0.2–0.7mm;
sparse well-sorted mica, 0.1mm.

Surface treatment
All vessels are wheel thrown. Mortaria bear white, grey and pink quartz grits and are generally undecorated, though one has a cordon with slash marks round the body (not illustrated). The 'parchment' wares are painted in red and brown scrolls and lines.

M3. Red/brown colour-coated beakers, bowls and mortaria

Fig 31.
Nos 211, 217.

Colour
Core, margin and surfaces orange/brown.

Paste
Hard, very fine.

Inclusions
Frequent well-sorted rounded sand, 0.1mm;
quartz varies according to type of pot – in mortaria it is frequent well-sorted rounded, 0.1mm, in bowls and beakers moderate – sparse well-sorted rounded 0.2mm;
moderate well-sorted rounded ironstone 0.1mm;
sparse well-sorted mica 0.1mm, except in beakers where it is frequent well-sorted 0.1mm;
occasionally 'T', a white crystalline substance, non-reactive to hydrochloric acid, is present: sparse well-sorted sub-angular, 0.2mm.

Surface treatment
Red/brown colour-coat; white slip decoration on rim and body of bowls; rouletting under rim on bowls; pink, grey and white translucent grits on mortaria.

M4. Red/brown colour-coated beakers and bowls

Fig 31.
No 210.

Colour
Core, orange/brown, margin and surfaces buff.

Paste
Hard, granular texture.

Inclusions
Frequent well-sorted rounded sand, 0.1mm;
frequent ill-sorted sub-angular–angular ironstone, 0.3–1mm;
moderate well-sorted mica, 0.1mm;
moderate to sparse well-sorted sub-angular–angular quartz, 0.4–0.5mm.

Surface treatment
Red/brown colour coat, no further decoration.

M5. White colour-coat mortaria

Fig 32.
No 223.

Colour
Core, pale grey, margin and surfaces orange/brown.

Paste
Hard fine to slightly granular.

Inclusions
Frequent well-sorted rounded sand, 0.1mm;
frequent well-sorted rounded black ironstone, 0.1–0.3mm;
moderate well-sorted mica, 0.1mm
moderate well-sorted rounded red ironstone, 0.2mm;
occasionally 'T' (see above, M3, for description) – sparse well-sorted angular, 0.2mm.

Surface treatment
White colour coat with pink, grey and white translucent quartz grits on interior.

M6. Red/brown colour-coated mortaria and bowls

Fig 32.
Nos 219, 221.

Colour
Core, pale grey–buff, margin and surfaces buff/orange.

Paste
Hard fine to granular.

Inclusions
Frequent well-sorted rounded sand, 0.2mm;
frequent well-sorted rounded ironstone, 0.1mm;
moderate well-sorted mica, 0.1mm;
sparse ill-sorted sub-angular grog, 1–2mm;
sparse well-sorted sub-angular quartz, 0.3mm;
occasional voids, 0.4mm;
occasional 'T' (see M3 above), 0.2mm.

Surface treatment
Red/brown colour coating only; grey, white and pink quartz grits on mortaria.

M7. *Colour-coated bowls*

Fig 31.
No 214.

Colour
Core, margin and surfaces orange/brown.

Paste
Hard, fine fabric.

Inclusions
Frequent well-sorted rounded sand, 0.1mm;
frequent well-sorted rounded black ironstone, 0.2mm;
moderate well-sorted mica, 0.1mm;
sparse ill-sorted angular voids, up to 1mm;
sparse well-sorted rounded 'T', 0.2mm (see M3 above).

Surface treatment
Red colour coat; rouletting below lip of rim.

N. NENE VALLEY COLOUR-COATS

Fig 31.
No 216.

Colour
Core, margin and surfaces white.

Paste
Hard, very fine, crystalline fabric.

Inclusions
Moderate well-sorted sub-angular quartz, 0.1mm;
sparse well-sorted mica, 0.1mm;
sparse well-sorted rounded ironstone, 0.1mm.

Surface treatment
Red/brown colour coating; barbotine decoration.

The postulated Nene Valley group has yet to be fully analysed but a complex picture is suspected. For a fuller discussion on the Nene Valley fabrics see Orton 1977, 41.

P1–2. COLCHESTER

P1. *Colchester rough-cast ware*

Figs 24–5, 27, 29–30.
Nos 50, 52, 57, 124, 126, 178, 192.

Colour
Core, margin and surfaces orange/brown

Paste
Hard, slightly sandy to crystalline.

Inclusions
Moderate–frequent well-sorted rounded ironstone, 0.2mm;
moderate–frequent ill-sorted sub-angular quartz, 0.2–0.5mm;
sparse well-sorted mica, 0.1mm;
sparse ill-sorted angular voids, 0.2–1.0mm.

Surface treatment
Dark red matt colour-coat; rough-casting with clay particles.

See also the report on colour-coat wares for further discussion of this group.

P2. *? A Colchester version of BB2*

Figs 24, 27–8.
Nos 39–40, 117, 153–4.

Colour
Core, mid-grey; margins, grey/brown to buff; surfaces, mid-grey to grey/brown.

Paste
Hard, very quartzitic fabric with a rough irregular fracture.

Inclusions
Frequent well-sorted sub-angular quartz, approx 0.4mm;
moderate rounded sand, less than 0.1mm;
moderate ill-sorted irregular particles of grog, up to 1.0mm;
sparse ill-sorted ironstone, up to 0.4mm.

Surface treatment
A thin slip overall which has been well burnished to produce a fine silky surface; sometimes burnished lattice.

This group of vessels occurs only in forms which copy the BB1 pie dish. In the absence of actual kiln material for comparison, it is not yet possible to confirm the attribution to Colchester.

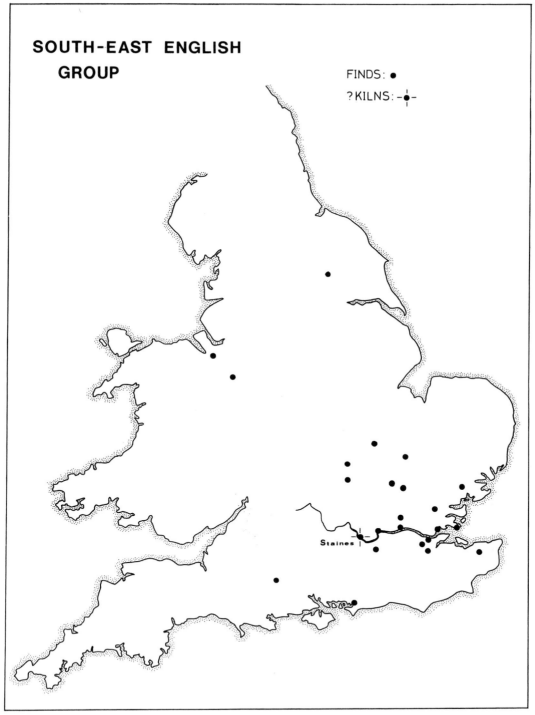

Fig 34. Distribution of Roman lead-glazed ware, south-east group

Q. UNKNOWN LOCATION

Fig 24.
No 48.

Colour
　Core, margin and surfaces grey–buff/grey.

Paste
　smooth, irregular, slightly granular.

Inclusions
　Abundant well-sorted round sand, less than 0.1mm;

abundant ill-sorted sub-angular quartz, 0.5mm or less;
moderate ill-sorted round grog, 0.5mm or less;
moderate well-sorted sub-angular ironstone, 0.2mm;
moderate well-sorted mica, 0.2mm;
sparse ill-sorted shale, 0.4–1mm;
sparse well-sorted angular feldspar, 0.5mm.

Surface treatment
　Mica-dusting.

There is only one form in this fabric, from Phase VII/VIII (14, the pond) (Marsh 1978, type 37). The presence of shale and feldspar may indicate a south-west English source.

R. UNKNOWN LOCATION

Figs 24, 30
Nos 49, 195.

Colour
　Core, pale grey; margin, orange; surfaces, orange.

Paste
　Very hard smooth fabric with a smooth fracture.

Inclusions
　Frequent well-sorted sand, less than 0.1mm;

moderate well-sorted sub-angular quartz, 0.5mm;
moderate well-sorted mica, 0.1mm;
moderate ill-sorted round ironstone, 0.7–1.0mm;
sparse ill-sorted calcite, up to 0.5mm;
sparse ill-sorted pale blue/green chalcopyrites, 0.2mm

Surface treatment
　Applied decoration, including arm; spout; rilling on the body.

This uncommon fabric, which occurs only in these rare forms, has not yet been assigned.

S. UNKNOWN LOCATION

Fig 27.
No 118.

Colour
　Core, mid-grey; margin, grey/brown; surfaces, dark grey.

Paste
　Hard, very harsh fabric with a roughly laminar fracture.

Inclusions
　Abundant well-sorted angular quartz, 0.3mm;
sparse ill-sorted irregular grog, 0.2–0.5mm;
sparse ill-sorted irregular limestone, 0.2mm–less than 1.0mm;
sparse well-sorted mica, less than 0.1mm.

Surface treatment
　None.

This unusual form is the only vessel so far found in this fabric, and it is not possible to attribute it to a kiln area.

T. PORTCHESTER 'D' (OVERWEY KILNS)

Fig 29.
No 173.

Colour
　Core, pink/orange; margin, cream; surfaces, cream/pink.

Paste
　Hard, harsh fabric, with an irregular laminar fracture.

Inclusions

Frequent ill-sorted sub-angular quartz, 0.3–2.0mm;
moderate well-sorted round ironstone, 0.2–1.0mm;
sparse well-sorted round black ironstone, 0.1–0.5mm.

Surface treatment
　Rilling on the body.

This fabric is very similar to that of the Verulamium region kilns (fabric H) but the forms and rilled body decoration are not found there. This fabric has been equated with the products of the Overwey kilns (also called Portchester 'D' after Fulford 1975a, 299). The illustrated vessel (no 173) was recovered from a late 2nd century level, which is much earlier than the 4th century date given for the kiln group (Clark 1949).

U1–6. SHELL-TEMPERED FABRICS

Six different groups have been defined within the shell tempered wares of late to sub-Roman date.

U1

Figs 29, 32.
Nos 175, 240–4.

Colour
Core, dark brown to black; margin, brown to orange; surfaces, grey/brown and red/brown.

Paste
Very hard fabric, with a smooth surface, and a roughly laminar fracture.

Inclusions
Frequent well-sorted sand, less than 0.1mm; frequent ill-sorted crushed shell, up to 2.0mm; moderate ill-sorted calcite, up to 1.5mm; sparse fossils, up to 1.5mm; sparse well-sorted mica, 0.1mm; sparse well-sorted ironstone, 0.2mm.

Surface treatment
Smoothed surfaces, probably wiped; occasional stabbed decoration, as no 243.

This ware is clearly made from a fossiliferous clay source. The results of current research on this will be published in the forthcoming report on The Hythe, Staines.

U2

Fig 32.
Nos 254–8.

Colour
Core, mid-grey/orange; margin, orange or pale grey; surfaces, buff/grey or orange.

Paste
Fairly hard, slightly 'soapy' fabric with a rough laminar fracture.

Inclusions
Frequent well-sorted sand, less than 0.1mm; frequent ill-sorted crushed shell, up to 2.0mm; moderate well-sorted calcite, approx 0.5mm; moderate ill-sorted red ironstone, up to 0.5mm; sparse well-sorted mica, less than 0.2mm; sparse angular voids, up to 1.0mm.

Surface treatment
All vessels have been roughly wiped to smooth the very coarse fabric, and one (no 248) has been pinched to form a frill at the rim.

It is very difficult to find good parallels for this ware outside Staines. It all comes from the late–sub-Roman black soil dated to the 4th and 5th centuries, and occurs in degenerate Roman forms (no 248 has a frilled rim, possibly an attempt to copy a tazza).

U3

Fig 32.
Nos 249–51.

Colour
Core, dark grey-black or brown-orange; margin, brown-grey or brown-orange; surfaces, grey-brown or orange.

Paste
Hard fabric with a smooth 'soapy' feel and a rough laminar fracture.

Inclusions
Frequent well-sorted sand, less than 0.1mm; frequent ill-sorted crushed shell, up to 2.0mm; moderate well-sorted calcite, approx 0.5mm; moderate well-sorted mica, approx 0.2mm; moderate well-sorted round black ironstone, 0.2mm; moderate ill-sorted shale/mudstone, up to 1.5mm; sparse well-sorted yellow/smoky quartz, approx 0.5mm.

Surface treatment
Surface wipe.

These vessels, made on a slow wheel, have been roughly wiped to smooth the surface, but are quite crudely made.

U4

Fig 32.   Nos 252–6.

Colour
Core, black/brown; margins, orange/brown; surfaces, brown/grey to black.

Paste
Very hard, slightly 'soapy' to the touch, and with a smooth laminar fracture.

Inclusions
Frequent well-sorted sand, less than 0.1mm; frequent ill-sorted crushed shell, approx 0.5mm; moderate ill-sorted calcite, up to 0.8mm; moderate ill-sorted ironstone, from 0.2–0.5mm; sparse well-sorted mica, approx 0.2mm.

Surface treatment
None.

Well made vessels in true Roman forms, all fast wheeled. The technique of manufacture is very similar to group U1, and since the fossil inclusions of U1 are absent here these may be local copies of the other group.

U5

Fig 32.
No 257.

Colour
Core, red/brown; margin, orange; surfaces, brown/grey.

Paste
Hard fabric, with a slightly 'soapy' feel and a rough laminar fracture.

Inclusions
Frequent well-sorted sand, less than 0.1mm; frequent ill-sorted crushed shell, up to 0.5mm; moderate ill-sorted shale/mudstone particles, up to 1.0mm; sparse mica, up to 0.2mm; sparse well-sorted quartz, 0.5mm.

Surface treatment
None.

Just one sherd in this fabric was isolated, and it may in fact be a variation of fabric U3.

U6

Fig 32.
No 256.

Colour
Core, light buff; margin, buff; surfaces, light grey/buff.

Paste
Hard 'soapy' fabric with a roughly conchoidal fracture.

Inclusions
Frequent well-sorted sand, less than 0.5mm; frequent well-sorted limestone, approx 2.0mm; frequent ill-sorted crushed shell, up to 2.0mm; moderate well-sorted mica, 0.1mm; moderate well-sorted black ironstone, approx 0.1mm.

Surface treatment
None

Several sherds from a single vessel in this fabric were recovered from the site. This very crude handmade vessel may be a local copy of more sophisticated types.

Groups U1–6 account for a high proportion of the pottery in late to post-Roman phases. They have no close parallels at other late Roman sites such as Shakenoak, where almost all the vessels have a characteristic rilling on the body, totally absent here (Brodribb *et al* 1972, 54–5, fig 23; see also Sanders 1973). This suggests that different origins and traditions were influencing the potters of the Staines shell-tempered wares. Although we have isolated six groups it is possible that in fact there are only three main groupings: (i) the fast wheel-made pots with fossil inclusions, U1 and U4, (ii) a slow wheeled localised fabric, U3 and U5, and (iii) the crude handmade vessels, U2 and U6.

Summary of the illustrated Roman pottery

Phase V, pre-Flavian (fig 23, nos 1–5)

The quantity of pottery from this phase is too small to allow any conclusions regarding potteries supplying the Staines market.

Phase VI, pre- to early Flavian (fig 23, nos 6–8)

This phase has the earliest mica-dusted vessel from local kilns at Staines. The presence of fabric H (Verulamium region) indicates that the kilns in that area were already exporting to a wide area in the pre-Flavian period.

Phase VIA, early Flavian (fig. 23, nos 9–18)

Nos 9–16 represent the group from pit 134, which includes several unusual forms alongside local types (eg no 9, a 'Haltern-derivative', and no 15, a 'Surrey' bowl).

Phase VII, Flavian–Hadrianic (fig 23, nos 19–25; fig 24, nos 26–47)

This is the first phase to produce a large quantity of material, of which the pottery illustrated is representative. During this phase the mica-dusted forms become more varied, and the majority are in fabric A, probably from a local kiln. The first 'poppy' beakers appear, of which two variants are illustrated. During this phase the Colne Valley kilns become more important, with many new forms produced, including a copy of a Verulamium region reeded rim bowl (no 34). The first Verulamium reeded rim bowls now rival the previously dominant 'Surrey' bowls. Also present are the earliest Dorset BB1 and BB1 copies; the first products of the Farnham/Alice Holt industry also appear, though only on a small scale. The colour-coated wares consist solely of rough-cast beakers, most of them probably made at Colchester.

Phase VII/VIII (the pond, feature 14), first half 2nd century (fig 24, nos 48–56)

The high percentage of Colchester rough-cast beakers and the scarcity of Nene Valley ware suggest a date before *c* AD 160. The samian and mortaria apparently confirm this as the date by which the pond was out of use.

Phase VIII, Hadrianic–Antonine (fig 25, nos 57–89; fig 26, nos 90–112; fig 27, nos 113–22 and 273)

The variety and quantity of mica-dusted wares found in layers after *c* AD 150, the accepted date for the end of the industry (Marsh 1978, 122), leads to the suggestion that, in the Staines area at least, the industry lasted until the 160s and perhaps as late as AD 180. The 'poppy' beakers provide an interesting range of forms, suggesting that some at least were made locally. The incipient flanged bowl in Colne Valley fabric appears at Staines during this phase, and may be a natural development from the 'Surrey' bowl rim form, which occurs in the same fabric. The Colne Valley kilns reach their peak in this phase, and a variety of forms are present (nos 82–95). The Verulamium region is the other main supplier (nos 96–110). Farnham/Alice Holt products are now present in greater numbers, though not yet the main ware they were later to become. The flagons in the Staines fabric may represent the final phase of the kilns in Staines.

Phase IX, Antonine (fig 27, nos 123–38; fig 28, nos 139–56 and 274)

During this phase the Verulamium region products predominate. The Lower Thames Valley group only account for 'poppy' beakers, and the mica-dusted bowl (no 134) may be residual. The Colne Valley kilns appear to be declining during this phase, allowing the domination of the market by the Verulamium region products and by BB1 and BB2 wares from Dorset and Colchester respectively. Mica-dusted forms are still found in fabric groups E and D, and as they occur in quantity and show little signs of wear it would seem reasonable to suggest the local kilns were still producing them. The complete absence of Farnham/Alice Holt wares should be noted. The presence of the Moselle Valley motto beaker confirms a date after *c* AD 160, and additional dating evidence is provided by a mortarium fragment from the Oxford potteries, dated *c* AD 120–180.

Phase IXA, late Antonine (fig 28, nos 157–62; fig 29, nos 163–77)

This phase contains material that is probably derived from Phase IX. The Verulamium region wares are still the dominant group, with Dorset BB1, and again there is a notable absence of Farnham/Alice Holt products. Mica-dusted forms are still present, but only in fabric D. The scarcity of Colne Valley products, which went out of production by *c* AD 180, confirms the suggested date. During this phase the first shell-tempered ware appears (no 175).

Phase X, Severan (fig 29, nos 178–89)

This group is associated with a building. The Verulamium region pottery is still dominant, and Farhnam/Alice Holt wares reappear (no 184). The last mica-dusted wares are present, all in fabric D.

Phase XI, 3rd century (fig 30, nos 190–209)

This phase comprises one large deposit, much of which was derived from earlier levels, and therefore only those vessels important for dating or not previously illustrated are shown. The presence of a number of colour-coated vessels, some (eg no 194) dating to the early 3rd century, and the absence of later 3rd century mortaria and colour-coats, indicate a date *c* AD 220–250/270. The presence of no 205, dated *c* AD 240–300, in the very top of the layer, suggests that, if the deposit is indeed of flood origin, it may have dried out after *c* AD 240 and occasional rubbish was subsequently trodden or mixed into the top.

Phase XII, late 3rd–early 5th century (fig 31, nos 210–35; fig 32, nos 236–58)

The pottery of this phase has a typical selection of late 3rd–4th century wares. The Oxford region provides the bulk of the colour-coat wares and mortaria. Grey wares come mainly from the Farnham/Alice Holt kilns, although the occasional pot in the Colne Valley fabric may indicate that there was still some production there. The range of shell-tempered wares is of particular interest, and indicates a number of sources of manufacture.

Residual pottery of special interest (fig. 33)

In addition to the stratified groups, a small amount of unusual wares from residual or post-Roman levels has been illustrated. These comprise lead-glazed wares (fig 33, nos 259–61; see also fig 34 and microfiche 31–2); mortaria (fig 33, nos 262–4; microfiche 32–3); a reeded rim bowl (fig 33, no 265; microfiche 33), a possible lamp (fig 33, no 266; microfiche 33); and painted sherds from an ?amphora (fig 33, no 267; microfiche 34).

Stamp and graffiti on amphorae

Amphora stamp

fig 35

268. Dressel 20, stamped handle. The stamp reads MCLSH, with an elliptical smaller stamp R.S below. This is apparently the same as Callender (1965), no 1043c, where the smaller stamp is more complete and reads PR.S. Callender suggests a south Spanish origin and a date in the second half of the 2nd century. Handle reused as a whetstone. (Phase VIII (36)).

Graffiti on amphorae

fig 36

All on South Spanish amphorae of form Dressel 20.

269. Body sherd with a group of shallow incised lines made with a blunt tool, possibly of wood, before firing, and of no apparent signficance. Orange fabric; the cream slip covers the graffito. (Phase VIII (36))

270. Body sherd with a series of curved, interlocked, heavily incised lines probably made with a wooden tool before firing, of no apparent significance. (Phase IXA (191))

271. Fragment of a handle with two deeply incised oblique lines, too fragmentary for further identification, and the numerals XII less deeply incised, all made after firing. Mr Mark Hassall comments that the graffito is probably contemporary and may relate to the quantity of contents in the vessel. (Phase IXA (191))

272. Body sherd with graffito incised after firing. Mr Mark Hassall confirms the identification of this graffito as (letter) A followed by (numerals) III. (Phase XVI (132))

Stamps on mortaria
KATHARINE F HARTLEY
fig 35

This report was completed by 1979 and therefore does not take account of subsequent research.

1. A mortarium in fabric H with a partially impressed stamp which, when complete, can be interpreted as Λ RIINTI.X retrograde, probably for some such name as Arentus or Arentius with X as a space filler. He worked at Brockley Hill (Castle 1976, 211 and fig 8, MS1–3) within the period AD 110–145. (Phase XI (10))

2. A flange fragment in fabric H with a partially impressed stamp, which can be attributed to the most commonly used die of Gaius Attius Marinus, who should not be confused with the maker of nos 6–8. He started his career at or near Colchester perhaps *c* AD 90, and moved for a short time to

Fig 35. Stamps on mortaria, nos 1–9, and amphora, no 268 (1/1)

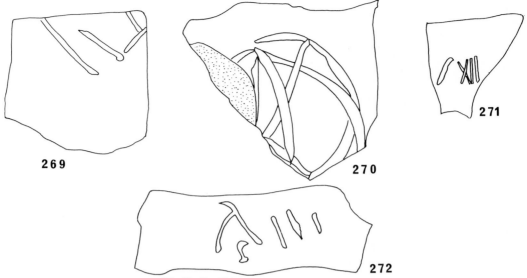

Fig 36. Graffiti on amphorae, nos 269–72 (½)

Radlett, Herts, where this mortarium was made, before migrating to Hartshill, Warks, where most of his productive life was spent (Hartley, K F, 1972, 373, no 12). His Radlett activity must have fallen within the period AD 95–110. (Phase IXA (53))

3. Two fragments, probably from the same vessel, in fabric H, with incompletely impressed stamps of Castus, who worked at Radlett and possibly at Brockley Hill within the period AD 90–140 (Hartley, K F, 1972, 374, no 15). (Phase VII (56))

4. A small rim-fragment from a mortarium in fabric H. The surviving border of a potter's stamp could well be part of a stamp of Doccas, but it is too fragmentary for certain identification (Castle 1976, 216, fig 8, MS9–12). *c* AD 80–120 (not illustrated). (Phase XI (10))

5. A fragment of a mortarium in fabric H, with a poorly impressed and incomplete stamp which cannot be identified with certainty, but is probably a stamp of Doinus (Castle 1972, 77, fig 5 Die D and nos 82–85). Doinus worked at Brockley Hill *c* AD 70–110, but Die D was probably his latest die, used *c* AD 85–110 (not illustrated). (Phase VII/VIII (14))

6. A flange fragment in fabric H, with a fragmentary stamp from one of seven dies probably used by one potter, Marinus. About 100 mortaria likely to have been made by him have been found at sites throughout Britain. He worked at Brockley Hill *c* AD 85–125 (Hartley, K F, 1972, 376, no 26). (Phase XVI (8))

7. A mortarium in fabric H (reddish brown variant), with a smeared impression of a two-line stamp from the same die as no 6 (not illustrated). (Phase IX (133))

	VIA	VII	VII/VIII	VIII	IX	IXA	X	XI	XII	Post-Roman phases	Total by source
Verulamium region	3	2	8	14	15	12	5	23	6	8	96
Oxford region					2		1	4	11	7	25
North Wales			1								1
Gaul/Kent							1	2			3
London/Staines				1	1		1	5	2	3	13
Surrey/Sussex									1		1
Southern England/ Northamptonshire			1							2	3
Nene Valley										1	1
Uncertain										2	2
Total by phase	3	2	10	15	18	13	9	32	20	23	145

TABLE 1. Sources and number of mortaria by phase (identified by Mrs K F Hartley)

8. A slightly burnt mortarium in fabric H (brownish variant), with an incomplete stamp from another die of Marinus. (Phase XI (10))

9. A mortarium in fabric H, with an incompletely impressed stamp, which when restored reads VDIIX retrograde, or VIDIIX (II for E is fairly common in mortarium stamps). This potter worked at Brockley Hill (Castle 1976, fig 8, MS 129–131 and 221). His rim-forms indicate activity within the period AD 90–140; neither this nor no 10 below could be earlier than AD 110 and are both probably later than AD 120. (Phase VIII (34); fig 26, no 107)

10. A mortarium in fabric H, with a fragmentary stamp from the same die as no 9 (not illustrated). (Phase IX (30))

11. A mortarium in fabric H, with a potter's mark in the form of a trade-mark. Only one other mortarium with the same stamp has been recorded, from London. The form and fabric indicate manufacture in the Radlett–Brockley Hill region within the period AD 110–145. (Phase XI (10))

The amphorae

O S FARRINGTON

This report was completed by 1979, and therefore does not take account of subsequent research.

C M Green, formerly of the Museum of London Department of Urban Archaeology, has kindly checked individual identifications in this report.

More than 62kg of amphora sherds were recovered from stratified Roman contexts; an additional 3.8kg of Dressel 20 sherds from later contexts have been omitted from the analysis. Very few sherds with diagnostic features, *ie* rims, handles or bases, were found, and identification rests primarily on fabric analysis at ×20 magnification of the hand specimen after the methods suggested by Peacock (1977a).

Eight fabrics were identified, associated with four or possibly five known amphora forms. An unusual number of graffiti was recorded for such a small assemblage, all on sherds of form Dressel 20. The earliest occurrence of amphorae was in Phase VII, of Flavian–Hadrianic date. The degree of abrasion and the size of the sherds varied widely, from severely abraded fragments weighing less than 0.05kg to large sherds of 2kg. Table 2 shows the presence of each fabric, and its associated forms where known, in each phase.

Dressel 20

This globular type comes from southern Spain, and was used to carry olive oil. The majority of amphora sherds recovered were of this type, 96.38% of all stratified amphora sherds from the site. Many sherds showed traces of a lining substance, probably pitch or resin, on the inner surfaces. Chop or cut marks were present on many of the surviving handle stumps and rims, evidence of secondary use. Particularly noteworthy was the number of cut-down rims, where the original neck and rim had been removed at the junction with the body. The new rims show clear signs of careful smoothing.

Dressel 30 (Callender 10, Pelichet 47)

This form made up 2.94% of the total stratified amphora sherds and was the second commonest form present, appearing in Phases VII–XII and residually in Phase XV. It comes from South Gaul and was probably used for wine (*cf* Peacock 1978). It is recorded in Britain in post-Boudican levels at Camulodunum and at Gloucester–Kingsholm, where it reaches a peak in the late 2nd century. How far the type persists into the 3rd century is not known, due to the lack of sites with firmly dated 3rd century contexts in Britain. This dating is consistent with the form's occurrence at Staines.

Dressel 30 first appears in Phase VII, and a peak is recorded in Phase IX, where Dressel 30 of all fabrics made up 5.47% of the amphora sherds recorded. The form certainly lasted into the 3rd century, but its occurrence in the 4th century at Staines is probably residual. One complete handle was recovered, the other sherds being identified by fabric analysis.

In addition to the South Gaulish wares, variants of Dressel 30 form were present in the assemblage. These were identified by fabric analysis as deriving from the Verulamium region, probably the Brockley Hill kilns, and as products of Staines kiln A. Two Dressel 30 rims of Verulamium region fabric (H) were recovered from Phases IX and X (fig 29, no 183). This form has not been identified amongst the Brockley Hill material, although the Verulamium region kilns were producing amphorae in the Dressel 3–4 forms in the late 1st and early 2nd centuries (Castle 1978).

It is possible that two further sherds in Brockley Hill fabric could have come from *Dressel 3–4* amphorae; both were neck sherds too fragmented to permit definite identification. They appear in Phases VII and VIII, pre-dating the Dressel 30 forms in this fabric. Amphorae from the Verulamium region were present in the four successive phases VII–X, and make up 0.56% of the total stratified amphorae assemblage. The Dressel 30 sherds assigned to Staines (fabric A) were only present in Phase XI.

Camulodunum 186

Only one example of this type was found, in Phase IX: it is a body sherd, and sub-type A, B, or C cannot be determined. Camulodunum 186 is of southern Spanish origin and was probably used for fish-based products. It has been found on sites dating to the 1st century BC, and variants of form 186C lasted into the early 2nd century AD (Peacock 1971; 1974a; b).

Graeco-Roman amphora (Rhodian type) (Callender 7, Camulodunum 184)

Two body sherds of this type were recovered, one in Phase XI and one in Phase XV. These contexts are respectively 3rd century and medieval, so that this 1st century form only occurs residually.

Amphorae of unknown provenance

1. Body sherd. Hard smooth texture, off-white fabric, close textured with occasional angular quartz, 5.0mm average, and occasional rounded red ironstone, 1.0mm average. The exterior surface shows rilling. (Phase XI (86))
2. Body sherd. Hard, soapy texture, off-white fabric, occasional angular fragments of quartz up to 3.0mm; frequent sub-angular quartz 2.0mm; occasional red and black ironstone, 1.0mm; and occasional limestone, 1.0mm. (Phase XI (143))

Phase	VII	VIII	IX	X	XI	XII	XIII	XV
Dressel 20	95.24	98.54	93.67	97.39	97.38	97.71	100	92.31
Dressel 30								
South Gaul	1.19	0.36	4.75		1.20	2.29		6.15
Staines					0.87			
Verulamium			0.72	2.61				
?Dressel 3–4								
Verulamium	3.57	1.09						
Rhodian						0.33		1.54
Camulodunum 186			0.86					
Unknown								
No 1					0.11			
No 2					0.11			

TABLE 2. Occurrence of amphora fabrics, assessed as percentage of total sherds (by weight) in each phase

The colour-coated wares

ANNE C ANDERSON

This report was completed by 1980, and therefore does not take account of subsequent research.

1st and 2nd centuries

Colour-coated beaker sherds with rough-cast decoration made up 50% of the total 484 colour-coated sherds. The majority of these vessels were manufactured at Colchester, and Colchester products are generally characterised by a hard sandy fabric, red in colour, with a darker, matt colour-coat (fabric P1 above). The dominant vessel form there was the bag-shaped beaker, frequently indented. Usually, the form of such beakers does not vary greatly (*cf* Anderson 1980, fig 13, nos 1–2) but the examples illustrated (nos 20, 50, 57, 124, 126, 178, 192) give an indication of the range of sizes and different rim types that may be encountered. The majority of the beakers have a cornice rim, which can be sub-divided into two categories: the first is simple, displaying almost no moulding (Anderson 1980, 35, Rim Type 1), the second heavily hooked, creating an overhanging ridge (Anderson 1980, 35, Rim Type 3).

Products from the Colchester kilns made up 40% of the total colour-coated wares recovered, the bulk of the material coming from stratified 2nd century contexts. This agrees with other dating for Colchester rough-cast beakers, which have been found on the Antonine Wall (Miller 1922, pl 49, nos 1–3; Robertson *et al* 1975, fig F53, no 17; Rae 1974, fig 21, nos 32–34) and on Hadrian's Wall in contexts dating to the earliest phase of occupation (Woodfield 1965, 114, no 28; Simpson 1913, 347, no 7).

Feature 66 produced a large group of rough-cast, bag-shaped beakers (fig 23), all derived from Colchester with the exception of one rim sherd of Continental origin (no 19). This latter vessel originated in the Lower Rhineland (Anderson 1980, Lower Rhineland Fabric 1). Petrological analysis supports this attribution, suggesting that this particular vessel was manufactured at Cologne. Such beakers were exported with other vessels to Britain *c* AD 80–165/170; this particular beaker is probably of Flavian–Hadrianic date.

Feature 10 also produced several sherds of Lower Rhineland Fabric 1, including the rim sherd of a globular rough-cast beaker with high curved neck and simple rim (Anderson 1980, Form 3). Such vessels date on the Continent to the period *c* AD120/130–180 and were exported to Britain largely in the Antonine period. It is apparent from the assemblage present on the site that Staines was well within the marketing areas of both Colchester and the Lower Rhineland.

Later colour-coats

The 4th century levels produced a high proportion of Oxford region colour-coat wares, largely made up of vessels imitating samian forms (fig 29, nos 214, 219). New Forest ware is represented by only one sherd (not illustrated), Staines lying outside the usual marketing area for New Forest products (Fulford 1975b, fig 55).

Mica-dusted wares

K R CROUCH

This report was completed by 1980, and therefore does not take account of subsequent research.

Five major groups, A–E, equivalent to A–E in the fabrics catalogue above, were isolated by microscopic analysis. Three of these could be equated with known kilns or production centres: A, Staines; B, Colne Valley South; C, Lower Thames Valley. The two other groups, D and E, come from localities at present unknown but probably both fairly local. Fabrics F, G and Q also include occasional mica-dusted vessels.

A total of 217 sherds was recovered from the site, in the following proportions: A, 10.5%; B, 19.3%; C, 32.7%; D, 23.04%; E, 11.05%; others, 3.41%.

Fabric	Date range	Form 7 (beaker)	Form 8 (dish/bowl)		Form 9 (jar)	Form 11 (lid)
A	Pre-Flavian–AD 130	59.0%	11.6%	23.4%	6.0%	
B	AD 100–180	12.5%	61.3%	26.2%		
C	AD 100–180	29.2%	37.5%	25.0%	8.3%	
D	AD 120/30–220	21.5%	53.7%	15.4%	7.1%	2.3%
E	AD 130–180	16.7%	45.4%	37.9%		
Proportion of total, each form		25.1%	44.0%	24.3%	5.6%	1.0%

TABLE 3 Proportion of forms produced in the major mica-dusted fabrics

The form numbers relate to the Staines form series and catalogue, available for inspection upon application (*cf* also fig 23, nos 6, 17, 18).

The low percentage of Group A (Staines region) is a reflection of the main date of the site, late 1st–late 2nd century AD, when the Staines kilns were going out of production. The low percentage of Group B (Colne Valley South) is similarly not unexpected; the kilns so far excavated there have produced only grey coarse wares. It is interesting that Group C (Lower Thames Valley) forms the highest percentage of the group. The same fabric has been noted at Brentford and it is possible that there is a production centre between Staines and Brentford. Group D (unknown location) is of particular interest as it produced nearly 70% of the bowls and dishes for the later period, of which 77% are the simple dish. Group E (unknown location) specialised in dishes and bowls in nearly equal proportions.

The simple dish was clearly the most popular product of the 2nd century kilns, whereas the bowl was more popular during the 1st century; this may reflect the quantity of bowls available in the 2nd century among the Verulamium region products and various black burnished wares. A major point which arises from this study is the duration of mica-dusted production in the Staines area. It has been generally accepted (Marsh 1978, 122) that the mica-dusted industry ended *c* AD 130–150, but in Staines there was still a strong tradition, especially of the simple dish form, until the end of the Antonine period or later. Group D is the latest of the mica-dusted wares, its disappearance coinciding with the decline of the town *c* AD 180/190–220.

Saxon and medieval pottery

PHILIP JONES
figs 37–8

A full analysis by form and fabric of the pottery used in Staines from the end of the Roman period until the 16th century is currently in preparation. As the material recovered from the Friends' Burial Ground contributes little to the general sequence contained therein, what follows here is a brief survey of the sealed pottery groups found in the dual concentrations of Saxon and medieval features to the north and south-west of the site. These remnant layers and truncated pits contained little datable pottery, and are mainly of value for the information they add to the general history of the site (see Table 4).

Within the deep overburden of late and post-medieval soils was found a much larger mixed assemblage of pottery which has been fully examined and recorded. The conclusions gained from this analysis have generally tended to confirm the main trends of pottery-working traditions found on other sites within Staines, for which the forthcoming type series will be the principal source of reference. Interesting aspects include the near absence of several known fabrics of Saxo-Norman date and the presence of some characteristically decorated early Saxon sherds in association with grass/chaff-tempered fabrics (fabrics MA1–3) in at least two features (120 and 111) in the south-west corner of the site.

Over 1000 sherds from post-Roman deposits were examined microscopically ($\times$20 mag), and also some from earlier features to clarify the relationships, if any, between late or sub-Roman fabrics and those of the early Saxon period. Of these, 792 sherds accord more probably with known Saxon or medieval manufacture than with any earlier types.

Abstract of the medieval pottery fabric type series for Staines

A brief summary of the full list of fabric types and their descriptions is presented here.

MA. SAXON CHAFF-TEMPERED FABRICS

MA 1

Hand-made; fairly hard; generally black, often with dull brown surfaces; variable thickness; smooth wiped surfaces that are occasionally burnished at the rim. Moderate to frequent amounts of chaff, with occasional quartz grains and rare chalk and ironstone fragments.

MA 2/3

Minor variants of MA 1 with either more or less chaff inclusions.

MB. SAXON SANDY FABRICS

MB 1

Hand-made; hard; pimply surfaced; black. Frequent inclusions of quartz (*c* 0.2–0.5mm) and moderate amounts of ironstone (*c* 0.6–1.5mm).

MB 2/3

Minor variants of MB 1 with either more or less quartz inclusions.

MB 4

Hand-made; fairly hard; well potted and of even thickness; smoothed surfaces. Micaceous body with frequent sub-rounded quartz grains (*c* 0.2–0.4mm) and sparse ironstone fragments. Black, with occasionally oxidised dull brown surfaces.

MC. SAXON GRITTY FABRICS

MC 1

Hand-made; hard; variable thickness; dark grey/black. Sparse inclusions of flint grits (*c* 0.5–1.5mm and occasionally up to 7.0mm) and more frequent quartz (*c* 0.1–0.3mm and occasionally larger).

MC 2

Hand-made; hard; harsh-surfaced; dark brown/black often with oxidised external surface. Moderate amounts of angular flint (*c* 0.5–1.5mm but often larger), frequent quartz, and sparse amounts of sub-rounded ironstone grains.

MD. LATE SAXON/EARLY MEDIEVAL CALCAREOUS-TEMPERED WARES

MD 1. Late Saxon shell-tempered ware

Slow-wheeled; fairly hard; thick-walled; mid to dark grey, with red-brown oxidised surfaces. Frequent large shell platelets and sparse ironstone fragments.

MD 2. Saxo-Norman chalk-tempered wares

Generally fast-wheeled; fairly hard; dark grey to black with grey or slightly oxidised surfaces. Two distinct wares identified:

   (a) frequent angular chalk fragments only (*c* 0.2–1.0mm),
   (b) frequent chalk and sparse quartz and shell platelets.

MD 3. Shell/chalk-tempered wares

Generally hand-made although occasionally wheeled; fairly hard; grey to black with similar or oxidised surfaces; pimply-surfaced. Frequent chalk fragments (*c* 0.2–1.5mm), moderate amounts of bivalve shell platelets, and gastropod shell fragments (*c* 1.0mm diam). Two sub-divisions identified:

   (a) calcareous temper only, and
   (b) with sparse flint and quartz grits.

MD 4. Black-faced shelly ware

Fast-wheeled; fairly hard; smooth-surfaced; mid-grey core with dark grey surfaces. Frequent inclusions of shell (bivalve and gastropod) and chalk, with sparse to moderate amounts of quartz and rare flint grits.

MD 5. Red/brown-faced shelly ware

Fast-wheeled; fairly hard; smooth wiped surfaces; grey core with red-brown surfaces. Frequent inclusions of large shell platelets (often up to 7.0mm long) and rare to sparse ironstone and quartz grains.

MF. LATE SAXON GRITTY WARE

Hand-made; hard; harsh-surfaced; mid to dark grey core with similar or oxidised surfaces. Frequent inclusions of flint and quartz with sparse to moderate amounts of shell and ironstone.

PHASE	CONTEXT	A1	A 2/3	B1	B 2/3	B4	C 1/2	D1	D2a	D2b	D3a	D3b	E	F	G1	G2	Ha	Hb	J	K1	K2	K3	K4	K5	K6	K7
XIII	117		1 (no 5)																							
XIV–XV	120/205	3 (nos 1&6)	3	2 (nos 2&3)	1	3 (no 4)																				
	121	2			1																					
	111	1	1	1 (no 7)			1											1			1		1			
	5	1	1		1				1 (no 11)			1 (no 12)		1 (no 9)			2 (no 10)	1			1	1	1			
	110														1		1									
	101	1																								
XVI	202	1 (no 8)																								
	27/18	4	2			2	1		1					1	1									1	1	1	
	3												3														
	1		1	1	1		1	2 (no 13)					1 (no 16)				7 (nos 14&15)	1 (no 17)	2	2		2 (nos 18&19)					
	17																	1		1			1			
	21	2				1	1									1	2 (no 25)	1 (no 24)	1	1	1		3	2	2	
	2	1									1				1		4	1		6 (nos 20–22)	4 (no 23)		3	2		
	38/39	4 (nos 26&27)				1						2	1	1 (nos 28&3)		1	3	1	1 (no 29)	8	11 (no 30)		6	6	22	4
Total no of sherds from stratified contexts		16	11	3	4	7	3	–	4	–	1	3	–	8	3	1	19	5	1	17	17	1	16	9	23	4
Total no of sherds on site		40	31	3	9	16	7	–	17	–	4	3	6	48	13	4	29	13	1	167	64	5	83	42	102	36

TABLE 4. Distribution of Saxon and medieval pottery fabrics (vessels illustrated on figs 37–8 noted in brackets)

MG. SAXO-NORMAN SAND AND FLINT-TEMPERED FABRICS

Hand-made and slow-wheeled; hard; pimply-surfaced; generally dark grey. Frequent quartz (*c* 0.4–0.7mm) and sparse to moderate flint and ironstone.

MH. SAXO-NORMAN TRANSITIONAL FABRICS

Occasionally fast-wheeled; hard; harsh-surfaced; dark grey with patchy red-brown to grey surfaces. Frequent quartz (*c* 0.4–0.7mm) and variable amounts of flint, shell and chalk. Two subdivisions identified:

(a) frequent quartz, with sparse to moderate amounts of chalk, shell and flint, and
(b) frequent quartz with moderate flint, and rare chalk and shell.

MJ. HERTFORDSHIRE REDUCED-TYPE FABRICS

Fast-wheeled; hard; harsh-surfaced; mid to dark grey, only rarely oxidised. Frequent quartz inclusions (*c* 0.3–0.6mm) and sparse flint and ironstone.

MK. MEDIEVAL SANDY FABRICS

MK 1. Grey sandy wares

Slow- to fast-wheeled; hard; sandy feel; generally mid-grey with reduced surfaces and occasional oxidised brown patches. Frequent sub-rounded and moderately well-sorted grains of quartz (*c* 0.2–1.5mm though usually 0.4–0.6mm) and moderate amounts of ill-sorted angular ironstone. Probably of late 11th/12th century date continuing into the 13th.

MK 2. Fine sandy wares

As MK 1 but finer, better levigated and potted and smaller quartz grains (*c* 0.4/0.5mm). Includes most of the glazed medieval sandy wares but in a variety of specific fabrics. Probably late 12th and 13th centuries.

MK 3

Fast-wheeled; very hard; sandy feel with metallic ring when struck; mid/dark grey with grey or oxidised brown surfaces. Frequent well-sorted and sub-rounded quartz grains (*c* 0.2–0.4mm) and sparse to moderate angular lumps of ironstone (occasionally up to 1.2mm). Fused ground. Probably late 13th/early 14th centuries.

MK 4. Ironstone/sandy ware

Fast-wheeled; hard; sandy feel; well potted from a good plastic clay, mid/pale grey with similar or often very pale orange/grey surfaces. Frequent sub-rounded quartz generally pink or red tinged (*c* 0.2–0.7mm though occasionally larger) and frequent angular ironstone fragments of metallic fracture (*c* 0.1–0.7mm and occasionally larger). Probably mid 13th–14th centuries.

MK 5. Surrey-type grey ware

Fabric as MK 6 but generally mid-grey with similar or oxidised brown surfaces. 13th–14th centuries.

MK 6. Off-white/buff Surrey ware

Fast-wheeled; hard; sandy feel; well potted; pale grey to buff or pale orange/pink, generally off-white but often reduced by soot-blackening on cooking pots. Frequent well-sorted and sub-rounded quartz, pink to red in colour (*c* 0.3–0.6mm). Mid 13th–14th centuries.

MK 7

Fabric as MK 1 but generally pale grey to off-white or pale buff in colour. 13th century.

The illustrated sherds

figs 37–8

Each figure number is followed by its fabric type, its context number in brackets, and a description of technique on decorated sherds.

Discussion

Since the reservations expressed in the first report on Saxon pottery from Staines (Jones & Shanks 1976, 101), sherds recovered from features 120 and 111 on the Friends' Burial Ground site have made it possible to postulate an early Saxon occupation with a higher degree of certainty. Both features produced grass/chaff-tempered sherds (MA 1) and finer pottery decorated with horizontal tooled lines and stamps on the shoulder. These finer wares are similar to those from other early Saxon sites of the 5th/6th centuries AD in southern England, such as Mucking (Jones *et al* 1968, 222), Portchester (Cunliffe 1970, 70, fig 3) and Walton, Aylesbury (Farley 1976, 168, 194–9, fig 13, nos 15, 17).

There remains much uncertainty about later pottery produced up to the 11th/12th centuries. Neither in the quantity of sherds nor in the stratigraphy of the excavated area, is it possible to discern anything other than general trends. Only a handful of imported sherds have been found with pottery of this period in Staines, red-painted pottery from the Continent of which only one sherd was found on the Friends' Burial Ground, in a residual context.

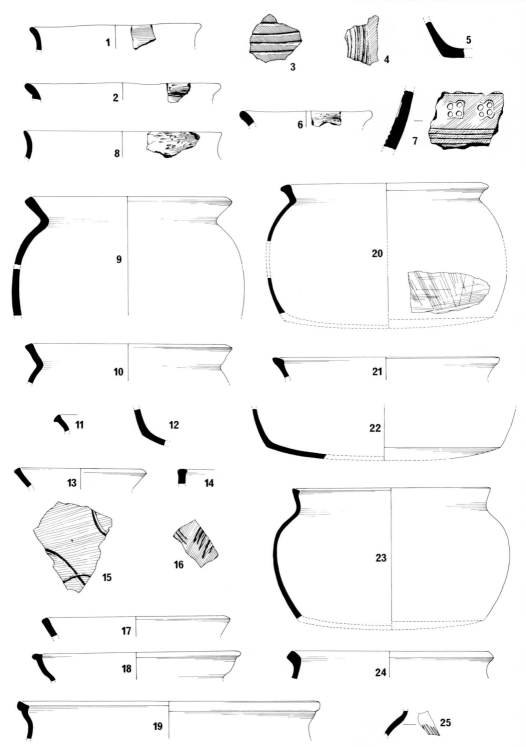

Fig 37. Saxon and medieval pottery, nos 1–25 (3–4, 7, 15–16 ½, rest ¼)

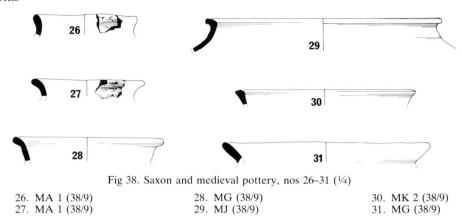

Fig 38. Saxon and medieval pottery, nos 26–31 (¼)

26. MA 1 (38/9)	28. MG (38/9)	30. MK 2 (38/9)
27. MA 1 (38/9)	29. MJ (38/9)	31. MG (38/9)

The dating of the pottery from pre-Conquest deposits at nearby Old Windsor (O'Neil 1958, 183–5) has implied that grass/chaff-tempered pottery was in use up until the mid-11th century and judging from the collections now deposited at Reading Museum, was accompanied for the most part by a coarse shelly fabric. Much doubt has been cast on the persistence of the grass/chaff-tempering tradition beyond the Middle Saxon period. In Oxford, situated on the principal highway of the Thames from London and established as a trading centre by at least the 9th century, these fabrics are absent. Staines does provide an earlier local date for grass/chaff-tempered pottery than do Northolt (Hurst 1961, 211–300) or Waltham (Huggins & Huggins 1976, 102).

The problems of dating early medieval pottery have been further complicated by the results of recent excavations in Oxford, with the establishment and dating of the St Aldate's type series (Durham 1976, 83, 176–90) which should lead towards a reappraisal of Saxo-Norman pottery in the Thames Valley. Simple or squared-end everted rim cooking pots, for example, so frequently considered to be of 11th/early 12th century date, as at Therfield (Biddle 1964, fig 20, no 4, fig 21, no 2), Winchester (Cunliffe 1964, fig 35, nos 13–15) and in earlier work in Oxford (Jope & Pantin 1958, fig 11, no C18.1), now seem also to have been produced much earlier. This would confirm some early dating put forward at Waltham (Huggins & Huggins 1976, 106, fig 36, no 19). Of the sherds illustrated here, this form is exemplified by fig 37, nos 9–10, and there are further examples from the overburden of the site.

1. MB 1 (120)
2. MA 1 (120) neck groove, possibly accidental
3. MB 1 (120) shallow combing
4. MB 4 (120) shallow combing
5. MA 3 (117)
6. MA 1 (205)
7. MB 1 (111) rosette stamps and grooved lines
8. MA 3 (202)
9. MG (5)
10. MHa (5)
11. MD 2a (5)
12. MD 3b (5)
13. MD 2b (1)
14. MHa (1)
15. MHa (1) incised curvilinear decoration
16. MG (1) shallow combing
17. MHb (1)
18. MK 4 (1)
19. MK 4 (1)
20. MK 1 (2) irregular and lightly incised scratch marks
21. MK 1 (2)
22. MK 1 (2)
23. MK 2 (2)
24. MHb (21)
25. MHa (21) combed decoration

Post-medieval pottery

SHEILA MORGAN
fig 39

This report was completed by 1979 and therefore does not take account of subsequent research.

The pottery considered in this report comes from pits 6, 7 and 125, all in Phase XVIII.

The catalogue is on microfiche 35–43.

The quantity of creamware sherds recovered is proof of the effect of Josiah Wedgwood's contribution to English ceramics – the production of a paste and glaze pleasing to the eye and hand and manufactured in such quantity as to make it economically available to all classes of the community. Dozens of other firms in Staffordshire were also producing it, in varying qualities, and finding it profitable. Lockett in his definitive book on the Davenport Pottery (1972) says that 'by 1794 creamware was becoming old fashioned' and yet John Davenport thought it worthwhile to buy and enlarge a factory at Longport, Staffordshire, in that year. Pit 7 contains evidence of his wares: again quoting Lockett, 'Light in weight, pale cream in colour, the ware is pleasant to handle and use'. Nos 1–7 are all part of a dinner service, simply decorated with two brown enamelled lines round the rim; nos 1–3 are all impressed with the early Davenport mark (no 2 in Lockett), *c* 1798–1815. The glaze on no 8, the Wedgwood impressed plate, is badly crazed (Towner 1957, 92, mark no 49), but no crazing mars the glaze of no 9, the Turner impressed oval dish (*ibid*, 97, mark 121). The Turner factory ceased production in 1806. These three important Staffordshire manufacturers all had showrooms and warehouses in London, so Staines inhabitants would have had no difficulty in buying their products. The impressed marks on nos 10 and 11 may be workmen's marks and not factory marks. The moulding on no 14 is similar to that on the handle of a fish server, illustration no 58 in the Whitehead catalogue (1798).

No 16 is an interesting survival of part of an early water closet. Lawrence Wright (1960) describes a pan closet: 'a hinged metal pan, when level, kept a few inches of water at the bottom of an upper bowl. When a handle was pulled the pan would swing down and the contents were supposed to be tipped into a cast iron or lead receiver and to pass into a trap below . . . The water closet of the eighteenth century might be of lead or even hewn from solid marble with a metal pan or plunger mechanism, *but towards the end of the century the upper bowl might be of glazed pottery*' [my italics]. On p 106 of his book is an illustration of a pan closet, which shows the upper bowl to have a flat inward turning rim and a flange two-thirds down the side of the bowl where it fits on to the receiver below. This exactly describes the form and shape of no 16. Unfortunately, there is no sign or mark of the manufacturer.

The unnumbered creamwares illustrate the wide variety of plate sizes and kitchen ware made from this material. A surprising omission from the creamwares are fragments of tea bowls, cups or saucers (no 13 is too small to hold a tea bowl or cup), all of which are illustrated in the manufacturers' catalogues. Our household seems to have relied on blue and white transfer ware for its tea-sets, as no 17 shows. The 'Bee Master' pattern is illustrated by Coysh (1970, no 155), possibly made by Wm Adams, 1819–64. The coffee can, no 20, has a handle very similar to the one illustrated in Whiter's comprehensive book on Spode (1970, 126), but attribution on handle shape alone is doubtful. The claim to Spode manufacture of the dinner plate no 55 is more certain, although it is unmarked. The quality of the printing, glaze and body is high, for which Spode is rightly famed. The 'Filigree' pattern was introduced *c* 1823 (Whiter 1970, fig 47).

No 21 is an example of ironstone china, a thick, heavy hard-wearing pottery introduced and patented in 1813 by C J Mason, and is printed with the 'Blue Pheasants' pattern (Godden 1971, no 24). This pattern was in production by 1818 (*ibid*, no 25). The pattern on the oblong plate, no

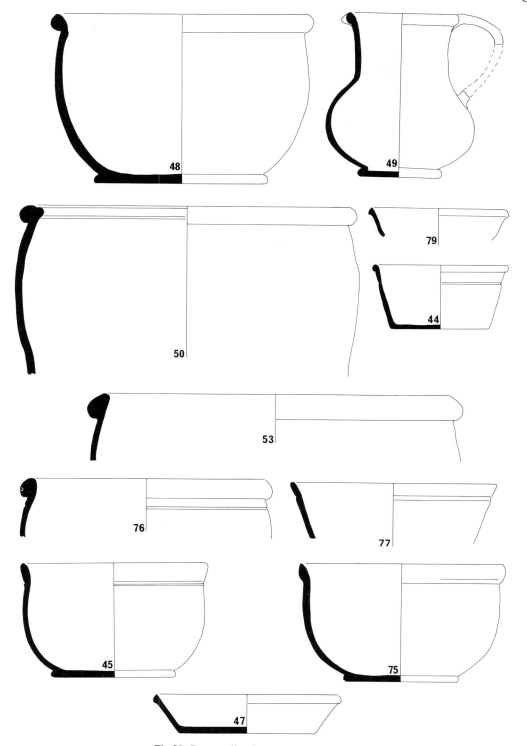

Fig 39. Post-medieval pottery, nos 44–79 (¼)

22, is identical to one illustrated by Coysh, marked Leeds Pottery and dated to 1800 (1970, fig 12). Nos 56 and 83 are both examples of the 'Wild Rose' pattern (Coysh 1970, fig 62), which was used by many potters and was only surpassed by the standard 'Willow' pattern in popularity. The three pits studied here have a representative collection of 'Willow' pattern plates, *etc*, showing marked differences in potting, glaze and printing.

Utilitarian buff-coloured kitchen ware is well represented, nos 33 and 61 having mocha decoration as well as coloured banding. This type of ware was introduced *c* 1800 and is rarely marked with the manufacturer's name.

Bowls nos 36 and 82 provide us with examples of two different methods of decorating. No 36, *c* 1825, has colour applied in broad bands, then horizontal and vertical lines incised through to the underlying cream body, making a very attractive square pattern. No 82 has colour applied to the cream body with a sponge, giving a mottled effect, very similar to the models of horses made at Leeds *c* 1790. Both bowls have moulded lines round the rim washed in green enamel.

In their attempts to whiten their creamwares the potters added cobalt to the glaze. The result was pearlware, pottery with a grey or bluey finish, depending on how much cobalt they used. Nos 58–60 are examples, 58 showing the common fine feather edge moulding enamelled in blue. Moulding of terminals of handles is often a clue to a manufacturer, and it is possible that no 60 is an example from the Rothwell Pottery, Yorkshire (Lawrence 1974, fig 7, no 7). In her notes on the excavation carried out at the site of the pottery, Heather Lawrence states 'mottled manganese splashed creamware was found . . . used in conjunction with green', so it is possible that bowl no 82 is from this pottery as well. Green edged plates, *eg* no 85, were also found on the site. This ware was in production *c* 1770–90.

All the stonewares were thick heavy pieces, with the exception of no 72, a fine white stoneware mug, decorated externally with a bright shiny blue glaze and a hunting scene in white relief. This particular type of decoration was very popular for mugs and jugs and was made by many firms. An illustration of the relief on a white unglazed stoneware jug is shown by Lockett (1972, fig 9). No 67's incised and rouletted decoration is similar to stoneware made in Nottingham.

The bone china fragments, nos 41–3, 73 and 74, all belong to the first quarter of the 19th century. No 73 is possibly a product of the Hilditch factory in Staffordshire. The pattern of a lady holding a lyre could be a version of the one described by Peter Helm (1975). The 'Broseley' pattern, no 74, was again made by many potters and without a mark cannot safely be attributed to any particular factory.

Of the coarse redwares, nos 47 and 79 appear to be similar to wares found on the Elmsleigh House excavation (Croft & Woodadge 1976). From the foregoing it seems that the date range of the pottery covers the period *c* 1790–1830.

Ceramic figurines

FRANK JENKINS
fig 40

This report was completed by 1979 and therefore does not take account of subsequent research.

All six figurines show the *dea nutrix*.

1. Fragment showing an infant supported on the left arm of the goddess, and suckling at the left breast. This is evidently part of a statuette of the goddess suckling two infants. Light buff clay with burnished white surface. (Phase XI (10))
2. Small fragment of the basket chair displaying the characteristic weave of the basketry. Light buff clay. (Phase IXA (53), not illustrated)

3. Portion of the neck and shoulder of the goddess with a trace of the fracture scar where the curved back of the basket chair has been broken off. Light buff clay with burnished white surface. (Phase VIII (197))
4. Two joining pieces, forming part of the flat D-shaped pad which sealed the base of a statuette of the *dea nutrix* type. The size suggests that it did not belong to no 6 below, but may well be part of a statuette of the

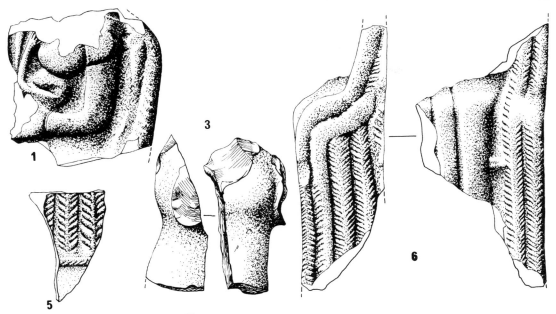

Fig 40. Ceramic figurines, nos 1–6 (1/1)

same size as no 3 above. Fine white pipe-clay. (Phase VIII (136), not illustrated)

5. Small piece from the back of the basket chair just above the base. Fine white pipe-clay. (Phase VII (169))

6. Fragment of the left side front showing the side and arm of the basket chair and a draped left knee. The folds of the robe skirt are represented by vertical parallel lines. Fine white pipe-clay. Three statuettes of the *dea nutrix* now in the Musée des Antiquités Nationales, St-Germain-en-Laye, have similarly folded skirts (accession nos 27952 (two examples) and no 7277, all found at Toulon-sur-Allier). There is also an incomplete example (in eight fragments) which was found at Snodland, Kent, and is now in the British Museum. All the others found in Britain have the folds arranged in a V-shaped formation. (Phase IXA (53)).

There are probably three versions of the *dea nutrix* type, two being in fine white pipe-clay, and the other in a light buff-coloured ware. The subject is a matronly personage, evidently a mother-goddess, in the act of suckling either one or two infants, while seated in a basket chair. Although the identity of the matron is unknown the name *dea nutrix* seems appropriate for the purposes of identification. A common and characteristic feature of the long series of this type of statuette is the basket chair. This has a rounded back which supports the matron up to the level of her shoulders, while the sides curve round towards the front to form the arms. All these chairs were apparently designed to stand on the ground on semi-circular bases without feet. Although the definition varies depending on the efficiency of the moulding and the condition of the original moulds, the woven wickerwork and the outlines of the vertical canes which support it are clearly discernible. There is also a band of plaited design outlining the edges of the back and sides. With two exceptions all the examples of this type of statuette found in Britain have the pattern of the weave indicated by short oblique incised lines arranged in herring-bone formation in vertical bands up the sides and the backs of the chairs. The pieces found at Staines display the basketry in this manner.

As the clay statuettes of matrons seated in basket chairs occur only in the series produced in the Central Gaulish *officinae,* and are not represented in the repertoires of the modellers who worked in the Rhine–Moselle industry, there seems every reason for regarding all the examples found in Britain, including the ones from Staines, as Central Gaulish products, most probably made at one of the several *officinae* located in the valley of the Allier.

Prior to the pieces from Staines coming to the author's notice, 52 examples of the *dea nutrix* type found in Britain had been traced. At present, however, only two of these are accompanied by information relating to the precise circumstances in which they were found and by details of associated archaeological objects. One found in a cremation burial at Old Welwyn, Herts (Westall 1930), was accompanied by samian pottery which according to B R Hartley should be Hadrianic or Antonine. The second example found at Arkesden, Essex, in a cremation burial (Jenkins 1958, 60), was dated by the late M R Hull to *c* AD 190–200 from the associated samian and Castor ware.

On the basis of this evidence one could assume that this type of statuette was arriving in Britain by *c* AD 125 and was still in popular demand as late as *c* AD 200. The latter date is misleading because the survival factor must be taken into account. Furthermore, the associated pottery may have been contemporary with the time of burial and does not necessarily indicate the date when the statuette arrived in Britain or how long it survived before burial.

The two fragments of the *dea nutrix* from Staines which have datable associated material were not found in funerary contexts, and therefore may provide a more reliable guide to date than the Welwyn and Arkesden pieces. No 5 came from a pit with pottery of a post-AD 100 date but no later than AD 130 on stratigraphical evidence, and no 3 came from the Phase VIII deposit dated AD 130–150/160. If the evidence from Hofstade (de Laet 1950) is taken into account it is clear that statuettes of the *dea nutrix* type were being manufactured early in the 2nd century AD, and that they were probably being exported to Britain certainly in the reign of Hadrian if not that of Trajan. On the basis of this evidence and that from Gauting (Kellner 1971) there are strong reasons for thinking that the statuettes of Venus should be similarly dated.

The glass

JOHN D SHEPHERD
fig 41

This report was completed by 1979, and therefore does not take account of subsequent research.

Roman vessel and window glass

One hundred and ninety-three fragments of vessel glass and 41 fragments of window glass were recovered from the site. Due to the fragmentary nature of the material only a few pieces warranted full description. The catalogue has been arranged according to the colour of the fragments, not in chronological sequence; this allowed all 234 fragments to be included.

Polychrome glass

1. Small body fragment from an unguentarium or small flask. Blown; decorated in band glass technique, with streaks of green-blue, white, purple and mauve coloured glass. Early to mid-1st century date, probably of Italian origin (Calvi 1968, 51, pl 6). (Illustrated) (Phase XI (10))

Monochrome glass

2. Small body fragment from a flask or jar. Blown; thin dark blue glass. (Phase XI (10))

3. Small body fragment from a flask or jar. Blown; decorated with marvered vertical trails of the same metal. Amber coloured glass (*cf* no 136 below). (Phase XII (28))

Colourless glass

4. Small fragment of rim and part of side of a beaker. Blown; rim thickened and fire-rounded, curving slightly inwards. (Phase XII (28))

   This fragment belongs to a well-known type of late 2nd–3rd century cylindrical cup (Isings 1957, 101, form 85), often on a low base ring, which occurs frequently among assemblages of that period. In Britain it is known as the 'Airlie' type after the fine complete example found at Airlie, Angus (Charlesworth 1959, 44–6, pl 1, no 4).

   The following three fragments belong to the same vessel group, but are in a naturally coloured dull blue-green metal.

5. Fragment of rim and part of side of a beaker.

Blown; technique and form as no 4. Blue-green colourless glass. (Illustrated) (Phase XII (11))

6. Fragment from rim of a beaker. Blown; technique and form as no 4. Blue-green glass. (Illustrated) (Phase XII (28))

7. Fragment of body, probably from no 6. Blown; technique and form as no 4. (Phase XII (28))

8. Body fragment from a beaker. Blown; decorated with a single horizontal wheel-cut line. Colourless glass. (Illustrated) (Phase XI (143))

9–11. Three fragments of colourless glass from thick-walled free-blown vessels. (Phase XI (143))

12–35. Twenty-four fragments of colourless glass from an indeterminate number of thin-walled free-blown vessels (Phase XI (143))

Green-blue glass (naturally coloured)

36. Fragment from neck and rim of a bottle. Blown; rim folded inwards and flattened outwards. Thick blue-green glass. (Illustrated) (Phase VII/VIII (14))

37. Fragment of rim of a bottle (or flask). Blown; rim folded inwards and flattened. Blue-green glass (Phase VII/VIII (14))

38. Fragment of the base of a bottle. Mould-blown; base decorated in low relief, with a cross radiating from a central dot. Each arm of the cross terminates in a dot and there is a similar dot between each arm. Poor quality pale green-blue glass with many air bubbles. (Illustrated) (Unstratified)

The existence of base designs on mould-blown bottles is well known (Shepherd 1978; Charlesworth 1966, 26) and this particular design has parallels at Harlow and Colchester (Shepherd 1978, Type XIII 6, 31, App II nos 272–5). These are the only examples of this design known to the author, and their concentration in south-east England, with the total lack of continental parallels, may indicate Britain as their place of manufacture, although with the present limited knowledge of Romano-British glass production this must remain a tentative suggestion.

39. Fragment of the base of a bottle. Mould-blown; the base is decorated in relief, but only part of an external square remains. Thick blue-green glass. (Phase XII (28))

40. Fragment of the base of a bottle. Mould-blown, fragment distorted by fire. Thick blue-green glass. (Phase XI (10))

41. Fragment of a plain handle of a bottle. Applied to a blown or mould-blown vessel. Thick blue-green glass. (Phase IX (133))

42. Fragment of a plain handle of a bottle, as no 41. Thick blue-green glass. (Illustrated) (Phase XII (28))

43. Small fragment from the handle of a bottle, as no 41. Thick blue-green glass. (Phase VII/VIII (14))

44–81. Thirty-eight fragments of thick blue-green glass from an indeterminate number of mould-blown bottles (Isings 1957, 63, form 50).

82–92. Eleven fragments of thick blue-green glass from an indeterminate number of free-blown bottles (Isings 1957, 67, form 51)

93–126. Thirty-four fragments of thick blue-green glass from thick-walled vessels of indeterminate number and form (*eg* free and mould blown bottles, flasks, urns, jars, *etc*).

As might be expected in an assemblage of this kind, the bottle, in both the mould-blown square form and the cylindrical form, represents a large proportion of the glassware retrieved; this must be due to the differential survival between thick and thin walled vessels (*eg* nos 44–126). However, the bottle is certainly common among assemblages of the late 1st and 2nd centuries. The main period of production was *c* AD 70–140, after which new bottle forms were introduced.

127. Neck and rim of a tall flask. Blown; rim folded inwards and flattened outwards. Neck tall and narrow. A narrow handle, of which only part of the upper junction end remains, has been applied just below the rim. Thick blue-green glass. (Illustrated) (Phase XII (11))

128. Rim of a flask or small bottle. Blown; rim folded inwards and flattened downwards. Blue-green glass. (Illustrated) (Phase VII/VIII (14))

129. Handle of a tall flask or jug. Applied to a thin-walled blown vessel. Handle plain except for a single vertical trail. Thick blue-green glass. (Illustrated) (Phase XI (10))

130. Fragment of the handle of a flask. Applied to a blown vessel. Thick blue-green glass. (Phase XII (28))

131–3. Three fragments from the necks of tall flasks. Blue-green glass.

These fragments, nos 127–33 (with the possible exception of no 129, which may belong to a bulbous jug form (as Isings 1957, 69, form 52a), belong to a flask form (Isings 1957, 72, form 55) probably manufactured in the Seine/mid-Rhine region, the peak of manufacture being *c* AD 70–150. The shape of the body is either spherical or conical, often decorated with vertical trails of the same metal, but it is not possible from these surviving fragments to identify the exact body forms.

134. Fragment from the rim of a platter. Blown; tip of rim fire-rounded and folded outwards and downward on to the body of the vessel to give a large tubular rim and a broad collar. Dull green-blue glass. (Illustrated) (Phase VII/VIII (14))

This particular rim form is not common. It belongs to a thin-walled platter or bowl (Isings 1957, 148, form 118), and rarely occurs in the repertoire of the western glasshouses. The metal of this example is similar to other vessels of this type (Hayes 1975, 120, no 468).

135. Fragment of rim of a beaker or flask. Blown; rounded rim, ground down with a slight ridge on the exterior. Blue-green glass. (Phase XVI (3))

136. Fragment from the base and part of the side of a jar. Blown; cut-out open base ring. Thin blue-green glass. (Illustrated) (Phase XI (143))

This example probably belongs to a distinctive jar form of the late 1st–2nd centuries (Isings 1957, 88, form 66c). Such vessels have a bulbous body and a broad collar and are usually decorated with

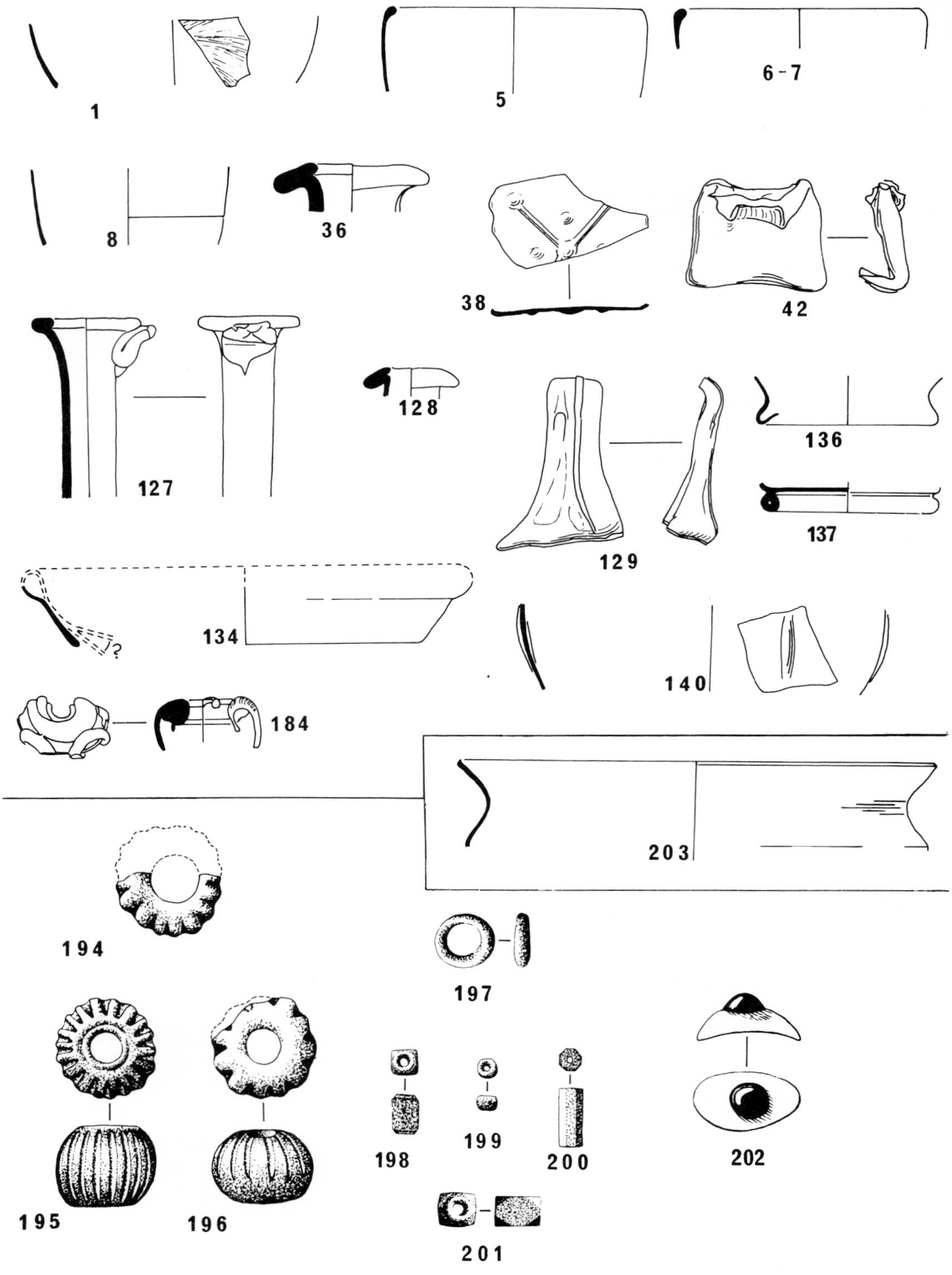

Fig 41. Vessel glass: Roman, nos 1–184, and medieval, no 203; Roman glass objects, nos 194–202 (½)

vertical marvered trails of the same metal (*cf* nos 3 and 140).

137. Fragment from the base of a bowl or beaker. Blown; tubular footring. Green-blue glass. (Illustrated) (Phase XII (28))

138. Base of a small bowl or beaker. Blown; simple thickened base with pontil mark. Green-blue glass. (Phase XI (10))

139. Fragment from the base of a bowl. Blown; slightly pushed in base. Thin blue-green glass. (Phase IXA (53))

140. Fragment from the body of a jar or flask (?). Blown; decorated with a thick marvered vertical trail of similar metal. Pale blue-green glass. The shape of this fragment indicates that it probably belongs to the bulbous jar form (see no 136). The trail, however, is much thicker and more pronounced than usual. (Illustrated) (Phase IX (133))

141–8. Eight fragments of blue-green glass from an indeterminate number of thick-walled free-blown vessels.

149–83. Thirty-five fragments of blue-green glass from an indeterminate number of thin-walled free-blown vessels.

184. Fragment from the rim and neck of a small narrow-necked flask. Blown; rim fire-rounded and broadened with a trail of glass of the same metal. A zigzag openwork trail has been applied between the rim and the body of the vessel, none of the latter surviving. Greenish glass. (Illustrated) (Phase XII (28))

As with no 134, this is another vessel type which rarely occurs in the western provinces. The zigzag trail decoration is similar to well-known Romano-Syrian styles of decoration used during the late 3rd–4th centuries, even in some cases surviving into the 5th century (Harden 1936, nos 493–8). This example, however, is probably of late 3rd century date.

185–93. Nine fragments of greenish colourless glass from an indeterminate number of thin-walled free-blown vessels.

Window glass

Forty-one fragments of window glass were recovered from the site, of which 39 are of the matt/glossy variety in blue-green glass. This type is predominant in the 1st and 2nd centuries, but does occur during the later periods which are characterised mainly by the double glossy type, of which only two fragments were found, both of greenish colourless glass. Much of the glass had mortar along the bevelled edge.

DISCUSSION

The glassware within this assemblage appears to represent two distinct groups.

(i) A high percentage of glass dated to the 2nd century, with one vessel (no 1) of mid-1st century date, and a few examples from the late 1st century. Also present were a relatively large number of window glass fragments of the matt/glossy variety.

(ii) A smaller group of vessel fragments which appear to belong to the 3rd and early 4th centuries, *eg* nos 134, 135 and 184.

It would therefore seem that the supply of glass to this site was interrupted probably at the end of the 2nd or the beginning of the 3rd century, as indicated by the distinctive 'Airlie' type beakers (nos 4–7), and was resumed in the later 3rd century.

Roman glass objects

Beads (illustrated)

194. Half of a cast melon bead. Blue-green glass paste with a glossy surface. (Phase XII (28))

195. A complete cast melon bead. Pale blue-green glass paste. (Phase VII (198))

196. A complete cast melon bead. Blue-green glass paste with a glossy turquoise surface. (Phase VIII (52))

The melon bead as a type is usually associated with assemblages of the 1st and 2nd centuries (Guido 1978, 100). From Claudian to Antonine times the true melon bead was imported from the Continent, but it was almost certainly copied by local factories in Britain.

197. Small circular glass bead. Blue-green colourless glass. (Phase IXA (191))

198. Small glass bead, rectangular, with chamfered edges. Blue-green glass. (Phase VIII (44))

199. Small circular glass bead. Blue green colourless glass. (Phase VIII (166))

200. Octagonal glass bead, chamfered edges. Dark blue glass. (Phase VIII (37))

201. Small rectangular bead with chamfered edges. Blue-green glass, (Phase XII (96))

Glass eye

202. Eye made of oyster shell and dark green/black glass, from bronze statue. (illustrated (Phase XI (10))

Medieval glass

203. Dark green fragment, thin walled vessel. Probably a prophylactic vessel, and probably a continental import of 13th century date (pers comm Dr D B Harden). (Illustrated) (Phase XVI (38))

The coins

M J HAMMERSON

This report was completed by 1979, and therefore does not take account of subsequent research.

Abbreviations

LRB=Carson *et al* 1965
RIC=various authors, *Roman Imperial Coinage* (London 1925–)

All coins bronze unless stated. State of wear, and therefore possible period of circulation prior to loss, shown thus: A=unworn, B=slight wear, C=average wear, D=quite heavy wear, E=very heavy wear, ?=heavily corroded.

Catalogue

1. Irregular copy, Claudius I. 23.5mm, type RIC 66, 'Grade IV/Grade III' copy. *c* AD 45–65, B. (Phase VIII (40))
2. Vespasian. Dup, RIC 743, Victory (Lyons). AD 73, E. (Phase IX (133))
3. Vespasian. As, illegible. AD 69–79, ?C. (Phase VII/VIII (14))
4. Vespasian. As, illegible. AD 69–79, E. (Phase VIII (36))
5. Domitian. As, RIC 335, MONETA AVGVSTI SC (Rome), AD 86, B (Phase VIII (52))
6. Domitian. Dup, illegible. AD 81–96, E. (Phase XI (10))
7. Domitian. Dup, illegible. AD 81–96, E. (Phase IXA (191))
8. Trajan. Dup, RIC 586, SPQR OPTIMO PRINCI-PI, Trophy (Rome), AD 103–11, C. (Phase XI (10))
9. Trajan. As, RIC 593, SPQR OPTIMO PRINCIPI, Victory (Rome), AD 112–17, D. (Phase XI (143))
10. Trajan. Dup, RIC 674, SENATVS POPVLVS-QUE ROMANVS, Felicitas (Rome), AD 114–17, B. (Phase XI (143))
11. Hadrian. As, RIC 617, PM TRP COS III SC FORT RED, Fortuna (Rome), AD 121–2, B. (Phase X (59))
12. Hadrian. Dup, RIC 973, COS III S C FORT RED, Fortuna (Rome), AD 128–32, B. (Unstratified (214))
13. Antoninus Pius. As, RIC 688(b), SALVS AVG, Salus (Rome), AD 140–4, B. (Phase X (155))
14. Antoninus Pius. Sest, probably Securitas (Rome), AD 145–61, D. (Phase VII/VIII (14))
15. Antoninus Pius. Sest, illegible (Rome), AD 139–61, C. (Phase VII/VIII (14))
16. Commodus, Sest, RIC 495, FEL PVBLICA PM TRP XII IMP VII COS V PP, Felicitas (Rome), AD 186–7, C. (Phase XII (28))
17. Uncertain. As or dup, probably 2nd cent, ?. (Phase VIII (34))
18. Caracalla (irregular). AR-plated AE copy of denarius. Illegible, early 3rd cent, ?. (Phase X (59))
19. Uncertain. Base AR denarius, very badly corroded. Rev possibly PROVID( ). Possibly Severus Alexander, ? AD 222–35, ?. (Phase XII (28))
20. Gallienus. Ant, RIC (Sole) 227, LIBERAL AVG, Liberalitas (Rome), AD 259–68, B. (Phase XII (28))
21. Salonina. Ant, RIC (Gallienus-joint reign) 7, VENVS FELIX, Venus (Lyons), AD 257–8, C. (Phase XII (16))
22. Gallienus or Claudius II. Ant, illegible, fragmentary, AD 253–70, C. (Phase XVII (8))
23. Tetricus I. Ant, RIC 57, COMES AVG, Victory, AD 270–3, C. (Phase XVII (8))
24. Tetricus I. Ant, RIC 103, PAX AVG, Pax, AD 270–3, B. (Phase XIV (20))
25. Urbs Roma. AE3, LRB1-200 (Lyons), AD 300, B. (Phase XII (28))
26. Constans. AE3, LRB1-142 (Trier), VICTORIAE DD AVGGQ NN, AD 347–8, A (Unstratified (213))
27. Constans. AE3, LRB1-149 (Trier), VICTORIAE DD AVGGQ NN, AD 347–8, B. (Phase XII (28))
28. Constans. AE3, LRB1-154 (Trier), VICTORIAE DD AVGGQ NN, AD 347–8, B. (Phase XII (28))
29. Constans. AE3, LRB1-159 (Trier), VICTORIAE DD AVGGQ NN, AD 347–8, B. (Phase XII (16))
30. Urbs Roma (irregular copy). AE 12×11mm, type LRB1-184 (Lyons), AD 330s–40s, A. (Phase XII (28))
31. Constans (irregular copy). AE 13.5mm, type LRB1-90 (Trier), GLORIA EXERCITVS (1 standard), AD 337–50, A. (Unstratified (213))
32. Decentius. AE2, LRB2–226 (Lyons), VICTOR-IAE DD NN AVG ET CAE, AD 351–3, B. (Phase XII (16))
33. Constantius II (irregular). AE 15.5mm, type FEL TEMP REPARATIO (horseman), overstruck on AE3 of Helena, type PIETAS ROMANA (*cf* LRB1-129), itself perhaps a copy. AD 350s–60s, A. (Phase XII (16))
34. Constantius II (irregular), AE 12mm, type FEL TEMP REPARATIO (horseman), AD 350s–60s, B. (Phase XV (5))
35. Arcadius. AE3, LRB2-167 (Trier), VICTORIA AVGGG, Victory, AD 388–92, B. (Phase XVII (8))
36. Lead communion token. Cross on obv, rev blank. Late 17th–mid-18th cent. (Phase XVII (122))
37. George III. AR shilling, 1816–20. (Phase XVIII (7))
38. George III. AR sixpence, 1816–20. (Phase XVIII (7))
39. Illegible. AE 10.5mm, ?. (Phase XII (16))

Summary

The coin patterns from the recently excavated Staines sites (Elmsleigh 1974, Friends' Meeting House 1976 and Central Area Development 1977) show differences which require examination together before we can draw conclusions about their significance for the archaeology of Staines. This will be done on the forthcoming Central Area Development report, and only a brief summary made here.

The irregular Claudian coin, no 1, could suggest a fairly early presence in the area. It is a copy of the common 'Minerva' type. The obverse is retrograde and very crude, and would qualify as a 'Grade IV' copy (Sutherland 1947, 155–60), while the reverse is slightly less crude, and engraved the correct way round. Whilst the occurrence of a single specimen should be treated with caution as regards the date of its loss on site, it may be noted that such coins were probably manufactured between *c* AD 55 and 60, though they seem to have remained in circulation until the end of the 1st century AD. Although Claudian copies are generally associated with the army or administration, it is unclear whether these poorest copies are of official manufacture or produced by the civilian population (Hammerson 1978, 588–93).

The unusually high proportion of Flavian (AD 69–96) coins, six out of a total of 31 Roman coins, suggests established occupation on the site during the last third of the 1st century AD, and the further eight of Trajan, Hadrian and Antoninus Pius (AD 98–161) show continued activity until the mid-2nd century AD. Between AD 150 and 250 coins are normally notable by their scarcity on British sites, and Staines is no exception; for a discussion of what this may signify, see Sheldon (1975).

In contrast, coins of the later 3rd and 4th centuries, normally common, are scarce; however, it would be safer to await the result of further excavations within Staines before it can be decided whether this reflects a decline in the settlement, a change in its nature, or merely a low survival rate for later Roman levels.

Individual coins of interest may be noted. The two copies of mid-Constantinian coins, nos 30 and 31, are both small and crude, the former particularly so; these types were commonly produced in Britain during the early to mid-340s, though it has only recently been recognised that they occur in great numbers, and that from 50% to 80% of the coin types of AD 330–48 are in fact copies. As with the Claudian copies, there is a possibility that they were produced by, or with the sanction of, the provincial authorities (Hammerson 1980).

Cameo ring

MARTIN HENIG
fig 42 and pl 1

This report was completed by 1979 and therefore does not take account of subsequent research.

Ring of copper alloy; simple hoop broadening out towards the shoulder, which is separated from the almost circular bezel by a moulding. The bezel contains a cameo of green glass in the form of a male head with projecting eyes and chin and straight locks which terminate in a fringe above the eyebrows. The hoop is somewhat corroded and a small section is now missing. The cameo has also sustained slight damage. Dimensions: external diam of hoop 20mm; internal diam 17mm; width of hoop across shoulder 4mm; width at narrowest point 1mm. The bezel measures 8×7mm, the cameo 6.5mm. (Phase IXA (53))

The ring may be compared with examples from Nor'Nour in the Isles of Scilly (Butcher 1967, 21–3, fig 8, nos 6, 9, 13; Butcher 1977, especially 43–4 and 56–60, where the original contention that the brooches were made on the site is rebutted). These are probably of the same date as the numerous brooches found on that site. According to the late M R Hull none of them need 'be later than the end of the 2nd century' (Hull 1967, 28–30). However, in the past, I have tended to

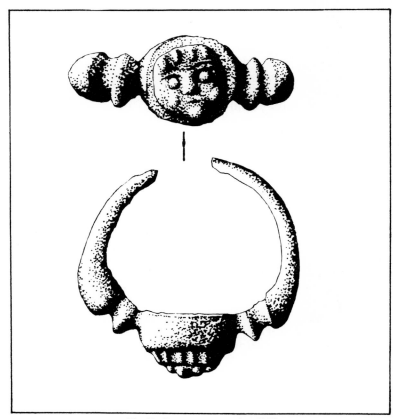

Fig 42. Bronze cameo ring (3/1)

regard little 'trinket-rings' with elaborate shoulders as being typical of the 3rd century (Henig 1974, 50–1). The Staines ring strongly suggests that, in many instances, this is too late and must reinforce the validity of the dating evidence from Nor'Nour. Other rings comparable to this one have been recorded at Gadebridge Park, Hemel Hempstead, and at Cologne and Kastell Pfünz in Germany (Neal 1974, 137, fig 60, no 115; Henkel 1913, 100, no 1078, pl 42; 120, no 1319, pl 50).

Cameos are extremely rare in Britain, so this is a particularly important find (Henig 1970, 339). The closest parallel is a head of Cupid on a ring made entirely of yellow glass (perhaps in imitation of amber) from Shakenoak, Oxfordshire (pl 1c; Brodribb *et al* 1971b, 106–7, no 153, fig 45, no 70). Most of the glass from the part of the site where it was found could be dated to the 2nd or 3rd centuries AD. This cameo might also represent a cupid, despite differences in coiffure; on the other hand we may be dealing with a debased and generalised 'portrait' as the straight locks recall the fashions of Trajan's reign (Toynbee 1962, 126, no 9; Babelon 1897, 175, nos 321–2, pl 38). The projecting eyes bring to mind the mask-like faces of late Iron Age heads, such as those on the handles of the Aylesford Bucket (Toynbee 1964, 23, pl 1, d). Such heads are, of course, found amongst native bronzes and statuary of the Roman period and it may be suggested that the Staines cameo is also of Romano-British manufacture (Toynbee 1964, 82, pl 16, d; 1962, 145, no 39, pl 39).

Glass gems of low quality were certainly produced in 3rd century Britain (Henig 1974, 164, fig 3). Here again, the Staines find is evidence for a local workshop at least as early as the late Antonine period (cf Henig 1969, 71–88; 1971, 215–30, for studios producing cut stones).

Pl 1a–b. Front and top views of cameo ring (3/1) (Photo: R Wilkins)
Pl 1c. Cast of cameo ring from Shakenoak, Oxon (3/1) (Photo: Ashmolean Museum)

The Roman brooches

D F MACKRETH
fig 43

This report was completed by 1979 and does not take account of subsequent research.

Colchester type

1. Length: 8.1cm. The original spring probably had eight coils but an ancient break has been repaired by inserting an iron axis bar through the remaining coils and mounting an iron pin on it; the corroded iron suggests that the pin was a length of wire wound round the axis bar. The right hand wing is damaged, but the left hand one seems complete and shows three flutes, the central one apparently having a small ridge in its bottom. The hook and bow are plain. The damaged catch-plate shows traces of two rectangular piercings and perhaps of another. (Phase IXA (53))

   This seems to be a standard Colchester type except for what may be a subsidiary moulding on the left hand wing. The ornamental characteristics of Colchester Derivatives start to develop on the parent type: the wings develop variant mouldings and the hook begins to receive more decorative attention (Down 1978, 277, fig 10.26, no 2, Claudio-Neronian), the bow's ornament tends to become more esoteric (Frere & St Joseph 1974, 42, fig 23.1), and the chevron is no longer formed by cold-working on the casting but formed in the mould (Down & Rule 1971, 47, fig 3.16, no 10). Most of these developments probably took place before the Conquest as the earliest Derivatives date from immediately after that event, and at least one type may well have been made before (see no 2 below). The Colchester dates from early in the 1st century AD to the Conquest in its pure forms and may have been made for a few years after in modified forms.

Colchester Derivatives

2. The spring is held to the body of the brooch by means of an axis bar through its coils and through the lower of two holes in a plate which projects behind the head of the bow. The chord is passed through the upper hole. Each wing has a groove at its end. The pierced plate behind the head is carried

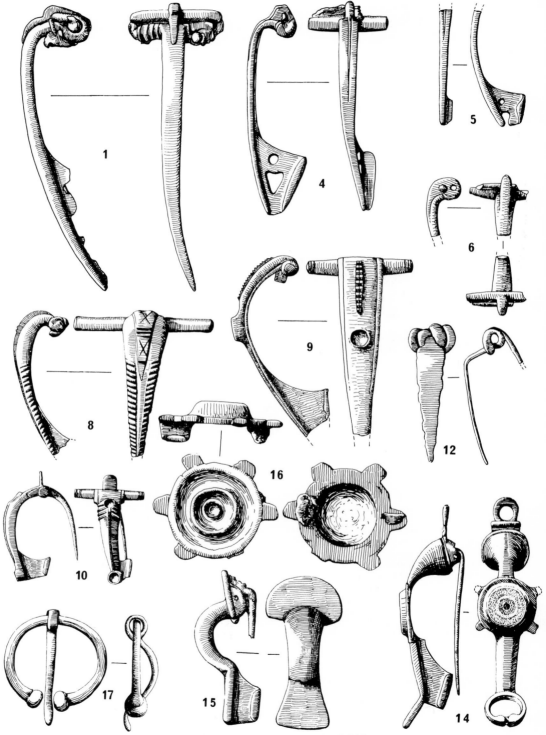

Fig 43. Roman brooches, nos 1–17 (1/1)

over on to the bow where it is finished off as a skeuomorphic Colchester hook. The bow has a flat surfaced ridge down the centre with a concave surface on each side. The catch-plate is sturdily formed with pronounced flanges on each side of the top surface with a cutout for the pin. (Not illustrated; Phase VIII (197))

3. The highly corroded head of a brooch of the same type as no 2. (Not illustrated; unstratified)

   This common brooch type is widely distributed over much of the same area as the Colchester. It is the only Colchester Derivative form present at Skeleton Green, Puckeridge, Herts (Mackreth 1981). Its stratigraphical context there was a little equivocal but there is a strong possibility that it should be dated before the Conquest. It seems also to be the only Derivative type recovered from the cemetery at King Harry Lane, St Albans (I am grateful to Dr I M Stead and Miss V Rigby for information in advance of publication). However, the type is present after the Conquest for at least two decades and the date range c AD 40–65 may be suggested for its period of manufacture.

4. The spring was held as in no 2. The wings are plain. The bow has a groove on the upper half running on to the start of the projecting plate behind the brooch which rises above the head, and two cross-cuts on the foot. The catch-plate has a small circular hole above a larger triangular opening. (Phase XI (10))

5. The head is missing, but the groove, with its bordering cross-cuts, and the form of the catch-plate suggest that this brooch was of the same type as no 4. The incomplete nature of the catch-plate may show that this is a faulty casting. (Phase XI (10))

   One specimen of this type was found at Central Area Development, Staines, in 1977 (report in preparation) and the arguments concerning its associations and date are fully discussed there. The date range appears to be fairly well fixed: late 1st century into the 2nd.

6. The head, minus one wing, of a brooch possibly of the same type as no 5. The head recalls that to be found on a small group which, at present, seems to belong to the southern Midlands; none is dated. The second half of the 1st century may be suggested, although the date range may extend into the 2nd. (Phase VII (67))

7. The spring is held as in no 2, except that the chord was brought up to pass through part of the bow rather than a plate or crest. The fragment is badly corroded and only the left hand wing shows any ornament in the form of two grooves at its end. The bow appears to be plain and most of it is missing.

   So little survives that no useful comment can be made. The date range may be the same as for the previous brooches. (Not illustrated; Phase VII/VIII (14))

8. The pin is hinged and the axis bar is carried in the plain cylindrical wings. The bow is hollowed out at the back and has on the upper part a raised strip which comes to a point at the bottom. The surface of the strip is ornamented with a raised moulding near the bottom, an incised saltire above, then three cross-grooves and, finally, another incised saltire on the head. The rest of the bow below the strip has a sunken ridge down the middle with a series of diagonal grooves on either side. The foot and most of the catch-plate are missing. (Phase XI (143))

   The closest general parallel comes from the Scilly Isles (Tebbutt 1934, 304, fig 3b), while another from the same islands has marked similarities in general design (Dudley 1967, 58, fig 23, no 229); neither is dated. All three belong to a limited development which can be described as a failed line of Headstud development. The early stages are best illustrated by two brooches from Hod Hill which show that the original sprung version of the brooch has the spring fastened in the Polden Hill manner: an axis bar passes through pierced plates at the ends of the wings and through the coils of the spring. The chord was held by means of a separate metal plate riveted through the bow and forming a rear-ward facing hook (Brailsford 1962, 11, fig 10, nos C100, C101). This stage had been reached by c AD 50 (Richmond 1968, 117–19). The rivet heads and the applied band became a vehicle for ornament (Wedlake 1958, 219, fig 51, no 11) and the feature remained after the hinged pin was introduced thus removing the original function of the plate (Spence Bate 1866, 503, pl 31, nos 5, 6); thereafter the ornament was part of the casting (Wedlake 1958, 221, fig 51, no 11c). The present brooch stands towards the end of this typological development. A few of the type have enamelled decoration (Dudley 1967, 40, fig 17, no 98) and all such belong to the end of the development. A brooch from Hengistbury Head (Bushe-Fox 1915, 61, pl 29, no 4) has the forward-facing foot-stud to be found in another family of what may be called failed Headstuds (see no 10) and it is likely that both sequences date to before c AD 75.

9. The pin is hinged and the section of the bow is as no 8. The wings are thin and each has at least one sunken moulding at the end. The bow is now in two parts and only the upper fragment shows clearly any details of design. There is a step down each side and a ridge in the centre, with cross-cuts on it, which runs almost down to a raised circular boss which seems to have a now discoloured enamel inset. The foot is missing. (Phase VII (33))

10. The pin is hinged and each wing has a sunken moulding at its end with a long projecting moulding flanking the bow. On the head of the bow is an upstanding plate with a rounded top, below which is a raised stud with a hollow centre, presumably for glass or enamel which is now missing, with four ridges running away on each side to the edge of the bow. Below the stud is a ridge with a series of hand-cut cross-cuts, running down to a forward facing stud, again with a hollow centre. (Phase XI (10))

    Both brooches, like no 8, are related to varieties which, by virtue of having a stud (usually enamelled) may be called Headstuds, although not part of the line of development which produced the familiar kind. The development of these alternative types probably followed the lines described for no 8. This shows more clearly on no 9, which bears a closer resemblance to the better known type. The main differences (as between nos 9 and 10 and another apparently related type: Tester & Bing 1949, 33, fig 6, no 2) lie in the form of the wings, and, as no 10, subsidiary mouldings, which belong to the more normal repertoire of Colchester Derivatives. Parallels for no 9 are hard to find, but for no 10 there appear to be related brooches in the south-west (*eg* Dudley 1967, 38, fig 16, no 86). The dates of nos 9 and 10 are probably the same as that of no 8, except for the presence of a projecting plate on the head of no 10. Although unpierced, this recalls the loop to be found with increasing frequency from the latter part of the 1st century, and may indicate that the date of no 10 runs a little later.

11. A fragment of the lower bow with most of the catch-plate from a Colchester Derivative. (Not illustrated; Phase VII (33))

Nauheim Derivatives

12. The spring has the usual four coils and internal chord. The bow has a flat section and tapers to a foot which is now missing along with the catch-plate. (Phase XII (28))

13. The spring and pin only from a Nauheim Derivative. (Not illustrated; Phase VIA (55))

     The Nauheim Derivative had a long life, devolving from its parent in the 1st century BC and, in Britain, lasting almost to the end of the 1st century AD, as the numbers at Fishbourne show (Hull 1971, 100, figs 36, 37: 21 Nauheim brooches to four Colchester Derivatives). The present example has no feature which would suggest that it should be considered pre-Conquest in date, therefore its range is likely to be *c* AD 50–80.

Trumpet brooch

14. The spring with an internal chord is held between pierced lugs by means of an axis bar. On the head is a cast loop on a grooved pedestal. The trumpet head is outlined by another groove and has a flat face down the middle. The central ornament consists of a raised boss with a blue enamel inner ring and a red outer ring mounted on a disc which had, arranged diagonally to the main axis, four small semi-circular projections of which the lower two survive. The lower bow has a flat central face and chamfered sides tapering down to an open peltate ornament. A well-made brooch which may originally have had applied repoussée decoration as well. This tends to corrode and its traces are easily missed. (Phase XII (28)).

     Despite the fairly large number known, the dating is not well established. One from Springhead, Kent (Penn 1957, 98, fig 14, no 5), comes from a deposit where the latest piece of samian was *c* AD 175. Another from Camerton, Somerset (Wedlake 1958, 224, fig 51, no 19), belongs to the end of the 1st century. The date is likely to be in the 2nd century, but the origins of the type are probably in the 1st, although perhaps not as early as *c* AD 75.

Unclassified bow brooch

15. The spring, with an internal chord, is held between pierced plates by an axis bar behind the semi-circular plate at the head of the brooch. The bow is hollowed out behind, has a swollen front, and springs from the centre of the lower edge of the head-plate. The bow has a flat fan-tail foot. (Phase XVI (8))

     An uncommon brooch, it is almost certainly an import from the Continent. It seems to be late: of two specimens from Richborough, one was found in the inner fort-ditch (Cunliffe 1968, 92, pl 33, no 84) and another came from a horizon dated to the late 3rd or 4th centuries (Bushe-Fox 1949, 118, pl 29, no 51). A related brooch made of silver was found in the Traprain Law treasure associated with coins, of which the two latest were of Honorius (Curle 1923, 5). The main difference between the present brooch and that from Traprain Law is that the latter has a narrow bow and the spring is mounted on a single pierced lug (*ibid*, 84, pls 32, 33, no 145). The probable date is late 3rd to 4th centuries.

Plate brooch

16. A circular brooch with a raised centre, heavily corroded. There is a small circular depression around which is a groove. The base of the raised area is separated from the rim of the brooch by a depression. Around the edge are six semi-circular projections; five survive. (Phase XVI (8))

     Several plate brooches have been found in Britain; one, from Kidlington, Oxon (Hunter & Kirk 1952–3, 57, fig 25, no 2), was found in a cache of brooches belonging mainly to the 2nd century. Another was found at Dura Europos (Cox 1949, pl 9, no 21), occupied by the Romans from AD 165 to 256, where it may have been a survival in use at the earlier date.

Penannular

17. The ring has a circular section. Each terminal is formed into a large boss separated from the ring by a small moulding. The pin is well 'humped' and has a longitudinal groove on the wrap-round on the opposite side from the hump. (Phase XVI (8))

     Penannular brooches tend to be easy to make and simple in design. The result may have been that their varieties had a much longer life than varieties of bow brooches. The dating evidence for no 17 suggests that the type was in manufacture for some time (Maiden Castle, Dorset, 150–100 BC (Wheeler 1943, 264, fig 86, no 2); Hod Hill, Dorset, up to *c* AD 50 (Brailsford 1962, 12, fig 11, E2; Richmond 1968, 117–19). In the latter case, it should be noted that there was extensive Iron Age occupation before the Roman Conquest and that the Durden Collection was accumulated from finds made after ploughing). The only notable feature of the brooch, apart from the terminal, is the pin, which has a fairly marked hump: an early feature. The date range for the type may run from the 1st century BC to well into the 1st century AD.

Objects of copper alloy

W PAINTER and S A SHANKS
figs 44–7

This report was completed by 1979.

We would like to thank Dr Hugh Chapman for his help, and Mrs A R Goodall for her comments on nos 52–3.

The finds of copper alloy, as was the case with most of the other small objects, were recovered in a good state of preservation. The context number is given in brackets following the description.

Roman objects

fig 44

Phases VI and VIA

1. A spoon-shaped spatula with decorative moulding on a six-sided shaft; other end lost. (176)
2. A knife handle (broken), of a distinctive Germanic type dated to the second half of the 1st century (Garbsch 1975, 71, no 4). British sites with similar knives include Verulamium (Waugh & Goodburn 1972, fig 35, no 75) and Nanstallon (Fox & Ravenhill 1972, fig 19, no 12). (176)
3. Part of a bronze ring (broken), irregular section, two sides bevelled. (55)

Phase VII

4. Bronze needle, broken at eye. (33)

Phase VII/VIII

5. Ligula/unguent spoon, the end of the handle flattened and indented to form a small spoon. Other end of the handle slightly bent. (14)
6. Twisted bronze wire, as used, for example, to attach steelyard fittings (*cf* Bushe-Fox 1932, pl 14, nos 44, 47). (14)
7. Bronze rod flattened at one end to form an unguent spoon. Small nick out of one edge. Circular shaft tapering at one end. (14)
8. Flattened bronze strip, one end cut to form a nail-cleaner, other end widened with central punched hole for attachment to bronze ring (see Barker 1976b, fig 24, no 4). (14)

Phase VIII

9. Bronze rod shaped to form hook, as used to attach a steelyard pan (*cf* Neal 1974, fig 56, no 47). (137)
10. Piece of a circular bronze sheet, with traces of a square-cut rivet hole. (137)
11. Head of a large round-headed pin, slightly corroded. (64)
12. Shaft of a needle or pin; head missing. (41)

Phase IXA

13. Probably the shaft of a needle or pin. (53)
14. A bronze strip with a circular depression at one end, possibly an unguent spoon handle. (53)
15. Strip of bronze shaped to form nail cleaner, with squared head and punched circular hole (as no 13). (191)
16. Shaft of a needle, pin or toilet implement, head missing, circular section. (53)
17. Piece of folded bronze sheet, central fold original. (191)
18. Bent round-headed pin. (53)

Phase X

19. Unguent spoon with moulded bead-and-reel decoration on hexagonal shaft. (141)
20. Part of a bronze needle, broken at eye and point. (59)

fig 45

Phase XI

21. Rectangular piece of bronze sheeting with two rivet holes, probably a binding from a casket or similar object. (143)
22. Curved bronze strip with rivet hole at one end, broken at other end. (10)
23. The two halves of a decorated bone knife handle with bronze strap fastening, no blade. (143)
24. Bronze pin with a decorated head of two roundels, broken tip. (143)
25. Bent circular bronze rod flattened at one end into an elliptical shape to form hook. (143)

Phase XII

26. Plain bronze finger ring. (11)
27. Small piece of bronze sheeting, slightly curved. (11)
28. Bronze wire with circular section. (28)
29. Thin circular plate of copper with slightly raised boss in centre and square-cut perforation, perhaps to take a rivet. A similar medallion comes from Longthorpe (Frere & St Joseph 1974, fig 34, no 102). (28)
30. Bronze armlet, the ends twisted to form a sealed spiral ornament. The small bronze attachment is adjustable, perhaps part of further ornamentation which is now missing. Parallels come from Richborough (Radford 1932, pl 14, nos 45–6; Wilson 1968, pl 41, no 156), where they are dated

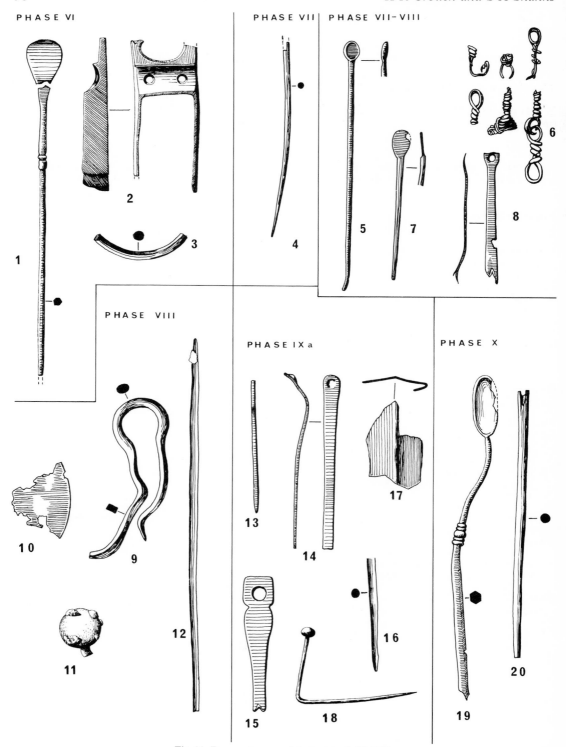

Fig 44. Roman bronze objects, nos 1–20 (1/1)

PHASE XI

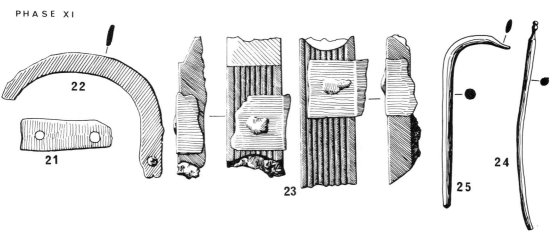

PHASE XII

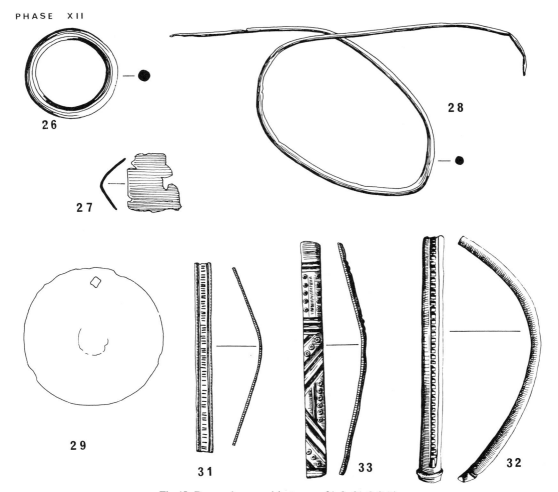

Fig 45. Roman bronze objects, nos 21–9, 31–3 (1/1)

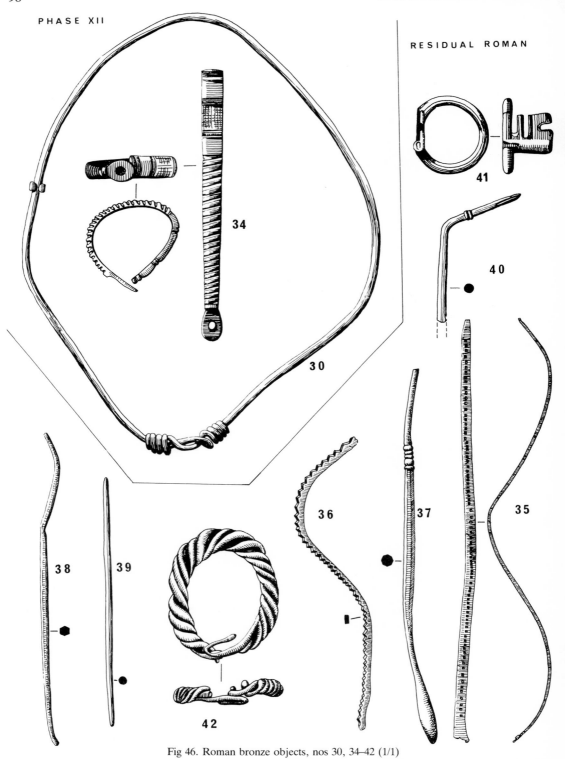

Fig 46. Roman bronze objects, nos 30, 34–42 (1/1)

RESIDUAL ROMAN

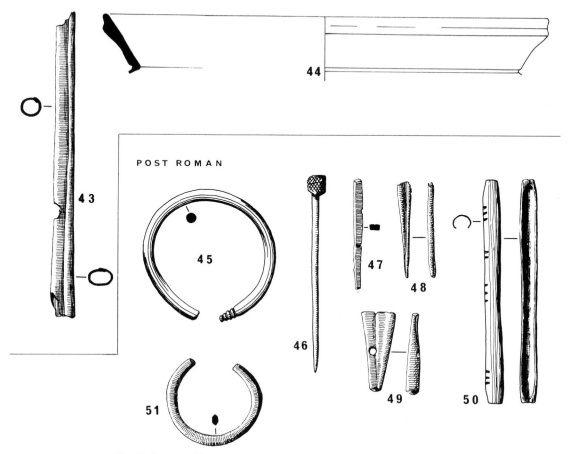

Fig 47. Bronze objects: Roman, nos 43–4, post-Roman, nos 45–51 (1/1)

after AD 330, and for which several German parallels are cited. (28)

31. Fragment of bronze strip decorated with central panel of indented lines, probably part of a bracelet (*cf* Neal 1974, fig 60, 135; Barker 1976b, fig 24, no 5). (28)

32. Part of a bronze bracelet with decorated panels of raised squares; broken at both ends, one at the terminal decoration. (28)

33. Part of a bronze bracelet decorated with a complex pattern of chevrons and circles. An almost exact parallel can be found at Richborough (Wilson 1968, pl 41, no 158). (28)

fig 46

34. Part of a bronze bracelet. One terminal is intact showing a loop fastening, broken in antiquity, and

bent, perhaps to form a small finger ring (*cf* Wilson 1968, pl 41, no 155). (28)

The bronze strip bracelets, nos 31–6, form an interesting group. The type does not occur in levels before the 4th century, and most were found in 28, the 'black-earth' deposit. Outside parallels for these bracelets have a similar 4th century date. Their distribution suggests that they are limited to lowland England, with concentrations at Richborough, Staines, Shakenoak (Brodribb *et al* 1971a, fig 30, nos 20–4) and Lydney (Wheeler & Wheeler 1932, 82–3 and fig 17), and others at Angel Court, London (Blurton 1977, fig 15, no 427), Enfield (Gentry *et al* 1977, fig 33, nos 15–16), Verulamium (Waugh & Goodburn 1972, fig 32, nos 32–4), Chichester (Down 1978, fig 10.38, nos 104, 108, 109), Gadebridge (Neal 1974, fig 60, nos 154–6) and Southampton (Cotton & Gathercole 1958, fig 12, no 8).

Post-Roman levels

35. Strip bracelet with punched decoration, broken at one end. (8)
36. Part of a bronze strip bracelet with saw-edged decoration. (3)
37. Spatula (spoon end missing) with a probe. Bead-and-reel moulding on an octagonal shaft. Similar ones occur at Gadebridge (Neal 1974, fig 63, no 196). (8)
38. Six-sided shaft of spatula similar to no 37, both ends missing. (8)
39. Small bronze rod with circular section, blunted at both ends. (Unstratified)
40. Part of a spatula with reel decoration, irregular section, broken at both ends. (3)
41. Bronze ring with a rectangular plate worked to form a key. (20)
42. Ear-ring of twisted bronze wire with hook and loop fastening (*cf* Brodribb *et al* 1971a, fig 30, nos 27–8). (8)

fig 47

43. Stylus case made of folded bronze sheet, broken at both ends (*cf* Cunliffe 1971, fig 49, no 134). (Unstratified)
44. Rim of a thick-rimmed bronze bowl, chamfered and grooved at shoulder. (Unstratified)

Post-Roman objects

fig 47

Phase XIII

45. Child's bracelet, with decorated spiral terminal ends (one missing); probably Saxon. (92)

Phase XVI

46. Bronze pin with head decorated in cross hatching. (8)
47. Small bronze bar with rectangular section. (8)

Phase XVII

48. Lace tag (aglet) of folded bronze sheet. (122)
49. Lace tag (aglet) of folded bronze sheet with punched hole in one edge. (122)

Unstratified

50. Bronze sheet rolled to form an open-sided tube with notched decoration on one side. (214)
51. Part of a plain bronze ring, with hexagonal section (214)

Phase XVIII

52. Four fragments of gilt chain with oval links, each *c* 4mm long (not illustrated). (6)
53. Fragments of thin sheet with irregular punched holes, possibly a patch (not illustrated). (6)

Objects of iron

K R CROUCH, P JONES and W PAINTER
figs 48–50

This report was completed by 1979.

The iron work was recovered in a generally good state of preservation. A representative group has been selected for publication. Context numbers are given in brackets.

Roman (KRC and WP)
fig 48

Phase III

54. Fragment of a hipposandal (not illustrated). (13)

Phases VI and VIA

55. Latch-lifter, rectangular section, heavily corroded at one end (*cf* Neal 1974, fig 71, no 395). (55)
56. One end of a hipposandal with one fastening hook surviving. (176)

Phase VII

57. Iron bar, rectangular section, fashioned into a hook. (56)
58. Split-spike loop. (56)
59. Iron blade, wedge-shaped section, broken at both ends. (66)

Phase VII/VIII

60. Wing of a hipposandal. (14)

61. Joiner's dog (not illustrated). (14)
62. Ring, circular section, with corroded attachment. (14)

Phase VIII

63. Tumbler-lock slide key, rectangular section, one end slightly flattened with roundel end and punched hole (*cf* Neal 1974, fig 71, no 382). (36)
64. Part of a hipposandal with one fastening hook surviving. (142)
65. Joiner's dog (as Frere & St Joseph 1974, fig 42, no 30). (58)
66. Iron plate (not illustrated). (142)
67. T-staple (see no 87; not illustrated). (44)

Phase IX

68. Saw-blade and part of surviving tang with one rivet

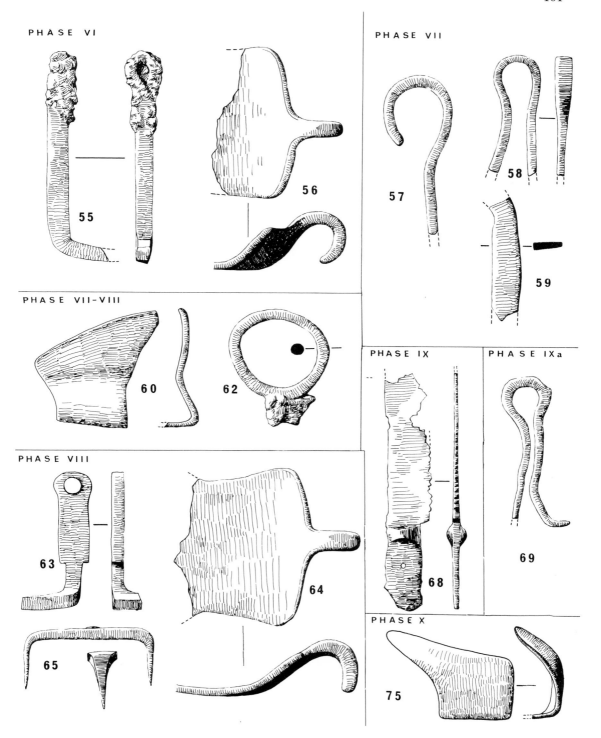

Fig 48. Roman iron objects, nos 55–75 (1/1)

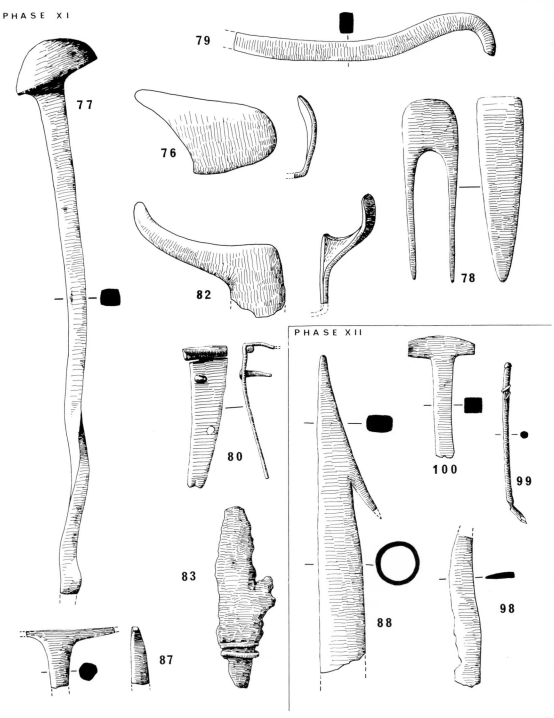

PHASE XI

PHASE XII

Fig 49. Roman iron objects, nos 76–100 (1/1)

PHASE XIII

PHASE XVI

PHASE XVII

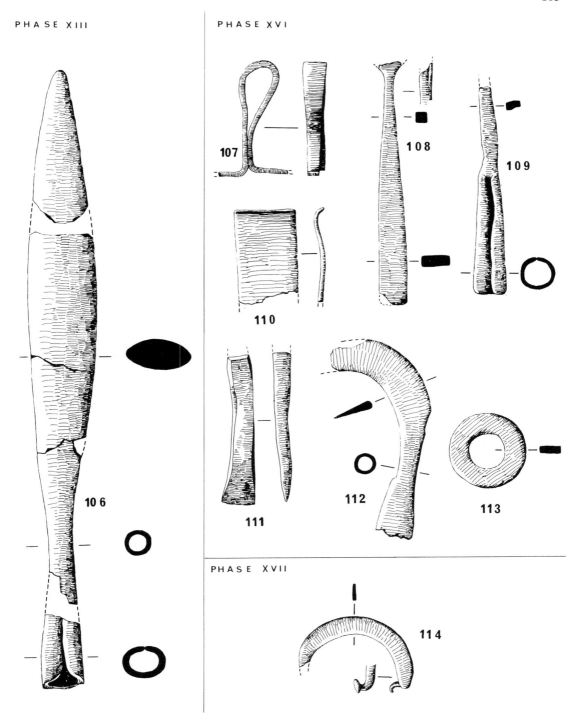

Fig 50. Saxon and medieval iron objects, nos 106–14 (1/1)

hole. Tang separated from blade by solid boss of iron (*cf* Frere & St Joseph 1974, fig 42, no 27). (130)

Phase IXA

69. Split-spike loop or ring-staple (*cf* Frere & St Joseph 1974, fig 44, no 45). (53)
70. Knife blade (not illustrated). (191)
71. Ring staple, as no 69 (not illustrated). (191)
72. Knife blade (not illustrated). (53)

Phase X

73. Iron plates (not illustrated). (173)
74. Staple (not illustrated). (173)
75. Wing fragment of a hipposandal. (173)

fig 49

Phase XI

76. Wing fragment of a hipposandal. (143)
77. Very large nail, shaft of rectangular section, a type used in boat building (Marsden 1965, 122–3). (143)
78. Large U-shaped staple. (10)
79. Rectangular sectioned bar with hooked end, broken at both ends. (10)

80. One wing of a hinge with one nail surviving and hole for a second. (10)
81. Iron plate (not illustrated). (10)
82. Wing fragment of a hipposandal. (10)
83. Knife blade and tang with bronze loop fitting. (10)
84. Iron blade (not illustrated). (10)
85. Knife blade (not illustrated). (10)
86. Head of split-spike loop (*cf* Neal 1974, fig 75, no 537; not illustrated). (10)
87. T-staple as used to hold box flue tiles (Frere & St Joseph 1974, fig 43, no 39). (10)
89–97. Heel and wing fragments of hipposandals: 89, from Phase VII (169); 90–1, from Phase VII/VIII (14); 92, from Phase X (59); 93–4, from Phase XI (143); 95–7, from Phase XII (28). (None illustrated).

Phase XII

88. Barbed spear with hollow shaft broken, possibly a fish spear. (16)
98. Knife blade, wedge-shaped section. (28)
99. Unusual stylus with wire spiral attachment with terminal boss in place of the more usual eraser. (28)
100. T-shaped tumbler lift key, broken at base, square section (*cf* Neal 1974, fig 71, no 382). (28)
101–4. Four hobnails (not illustrated). (28)
105. Knife blade (not illustrated). (28)

Saxon and Medieval (PJ)
fig 50

Ian H Goodall has kindly commented on nos 106–7, 110, 112–14. The broken implements nos 107–9 and 111 were found together in Phase XVI and probably represent a scrap-metal hoard which may also be associated with the slag detritus found throughout the layers of this phase.

Phase XIII

106. Spearhead with leaf-shaped blade and short socket. *Cf* Swanton 1973, series C2. (16; from very top of layer)

Phase XVI

107. Ring-headed staple with out-turned arms. (8)
108. Handle, possibly from a ladle or spoon, rectangular section tapering to square section at broken end. (8)
109. Iron implement with socketed shaft. (8)
110. Strap hinge fragment. (8)

111. Iron bar, rectangular section, tapering to form chisel blade. (8)
112. Socketed reaping hook, wedge-shaped blade on circular shaft, broken at both ends. (8)
113. Ring with rectangular section. (8)

Phase XVII

114. Hinged U-shaped shackle, one end broken, from a padlock with a sliding bolt. Such padlocks, introduced during the late medieval period, were opened by a revolving key, much like some globular padlocks from Chingley Forge, Kent (Crossley 1975, fig 35, nos 102–3). (122)

Objects of lead

W PAINTER
fig 51

This report was completed by 1979.

115. Circular lead disc with central punched hole. (Phase VIII (197))

116. Lead stud, (Phase XVI (2))

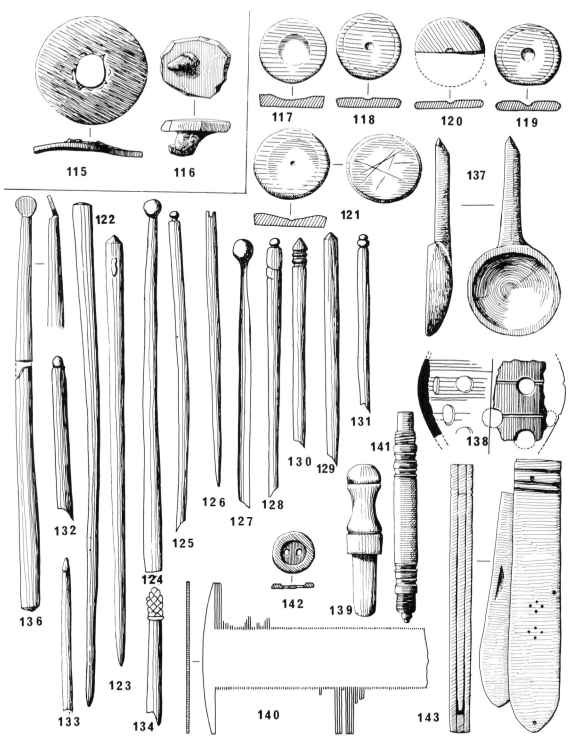

Fig 51. Objects of lead, nos 115–16, and bone, nos 117–43 (1/1)

Objects of bone and ivory

S A SHANKS
figs 51–2

This report was completed by 1979.

Context numbers are given in brackets.

Roman bone objects

GAMING COUNTERS

Phase VII/VIII

117. Bone gaming counter with central depression on upper surface. (14)

Phase IXA

118. Gaming counter with central turning hole and groove near outer edge. (53)

119. Gaming counter with central turning hole and groove at outer edge, worn on one edge. (53)

Phase XI

120. Bone gaming counter with central turning hole. (10)

Phase XII

121. Gaming counter with central depression, shallow

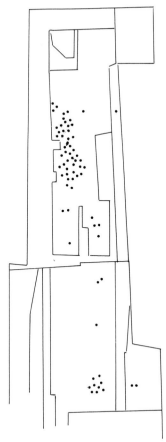

Fig 52. Distribution of Roman bone pins on the site

turning hole on upper surface and scratch marks on base. (28)

BONE PINS

A large collection of bone hair pins and needles was recovered from the site, mainly concentrated in the fill of the pond (14) and in one of the ditches (233) and the area surrounding it (see fig 52). Almost all, therefore, come from Phases VII–VIII (*c* AD 80–150/60), with the exception of nos 124 and 127 from Phase XII (AD 250/70–410/20). This compares well with the evidence from Colchester (Crummy 1979). All the artefacts were finished articles, indicating that this was not a manufacturing area, but it is not possible to draw further conclusions.

122. Large plain bone pin/needle (one example).
123. Complete bone needle with double bored eye and conical head (one example).
124. Bone pin with plain spherical head, broken at point (one example).
125. Bone pin with carved terminal in form of small boss on short neck, broken (one example).
126. Bone needle, broken at eye (two examples).
127. Bone pin, with chamfered shaft and spherical head (two examples).
128. Bone pin, the end of the shaft having a spiral groove ending in a plain boss head (one example).
129. Bone pin, plain conical head (two examples).
130. Bone pin, the end of the shaft decorated with two grooves and a conical head (26 examples).
131. Bone pin, decorated head with two bosses (one example).
132 Bone pin, simple decorated head (one example).

133. Bone pin, simple pointed head with single groove (one example).
134. Bone pin, pine cone decorated head (one example).
135. 28 broken pins, unclassifiable (none illustrated).

OTHER ROMAN BONE ARTEFACTS

Phase VIII

136. Ligula/unguent spoon, similar to no 7 in finds of copper alloys. (36)

Phase IXA

137. Bone spoon, handle deliberately broken and shaped to a point. (53)

Phase XI

See no 23 (finds of copper alloy) for a bone knife handle.

Unstratified

138. Part of bone globular cup decorated with drilled through holes.

Medieval and later bone and ivory objects

Phase XVII

139. Turned bone peg, perhaps from a musical instrument. (122)

Phase XVIII

140. Double-sided nit-comb, broken at one end, most teeth missing, no decoration. (7)
141. Turned ivory lace bobbin. (7)
142. Bone button, two holes in a central recess. (7)
143. Bone pen-knife, probably a letter opener. (7)

Shale artefacts

K R CROUCH
fig 53

This report was completed by 1979.

144. Half a shale bracelet, with irregular section, no decoration. (Phase IX (35))
145. Part of a shale bracelet, no decoration. (Phase VIII (36))
146. Part of shale bracelet, no decoration. (Phase XII (28))

147. A shale platter (*cf* Lawson 1976, 259–62). (Phase VII/VIII (14))

These artefacts, all of Kimmeridge shale, come from well-stratified Roman levels, and represent part of the extensive trade with the Dorset area in the Roman period.

Baked clay artefacts

K R CROUCH
fig 53

This report was completed by 1979.

148. Roman potsherd roughly shaped to act as a spindle whorl. Central hole bored from both sides. (Phase XI (10))
149. Baked clay loom weight, from a late Roman/sub-Roman well. (Phase XII (100))
150. Baked clay spindle whorl with incised decoration. (Phase XVI (8))
155. Baked clay loomweight. (Unstratifed)

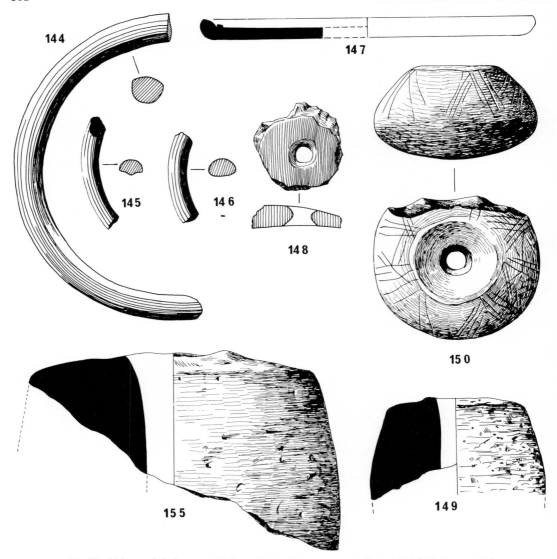

Fig 53. Objects of shale, nos 144–7, and baked clay, nos 148–50 and 155 (147 ½, rest 1/1)

Whetstones

K R CROUCH
fig 54

This report was completed by 1979.

151. Micaceous sandstone of a similar shape and stone to no 152, and presumably, therefore, of the same date. (Unstratified)

152. Micaceous sandstone. (Phase VII/VIII (14))
153. Micaceous schist. (Phase XVI (8))
154. Micaceous schist. (Phase VII/VIII (14))

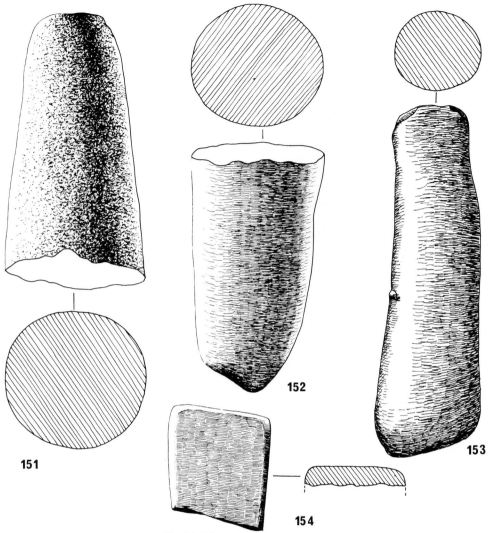

Fig 54. Whetstones, nos 151–4 (1/1)

Querns

H CHAPMAN
fig 55

This report was completed by 1979.

1. Fragment of heavily worn top stone of Mayen lava. (Phase VII/VIII (14))
2. Fragment of top stone of Mayen lava. (Phase VIII (36))
3. Quarter of a top stone of a quern in millstone grit or sandstone. Four fragments of the bottom stone of the same quern also present (not illustrated). (Phase XII (100))

4. Two fragments of a hard grey/black metamorphic rock, parts of the same quern (not illustrated). (Phase XII (28))

Of the 29 quernstone fragments found on the site, 22 were of basaltic lava from the Mayen area of Germany; this is a similar proportion to that found on the Elmsleigh House site (Chapman 1976, 127).

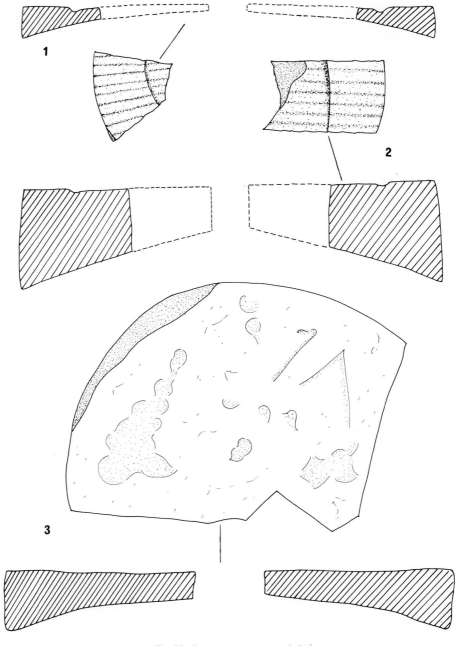

Fig 55. Quernstones, nos 1–3 (¼)

Building materials

K R CROUCH and S A SHANKS
figs 56–7

This report was completed by 1979.

The Roman wall plaster

Over 70 fragments of wall plaster were recovered from phases dating between *c* AD 80 and 410/420, but as nearly 50% of this comes from phases IX–XI, *c* AD 160–250/270, it would seem to fit best with the demolition of the Phase VIII building. This lends support to the suggestion that the building may have been a large town house, with many of the rooms in it plastered and decorated. The plaster is mostly plain white or red, but there are a few fragments with a trailing vine or floral design, none large enough to warrant illustration.

Chemical analysis shows that the plaster itself was made from local materials (possibly from Taplow, where the materials occur naturally), but that the paint was pure red ochre from an unknown source. Thanks are due to Mrs A Anderson for the analysis of the plaster at Leicester University.

Building stone

A variety of building stone was recovered from the site, all from phases later than VIII.

The presence of limestone blocks and Purbeck marble finishing slabs adds support to the evidence of the other building materials which suggests that a large town house was located in the vicinity *c* AD 150; since much of the building stone came from Phase XI (10), demolition before this phase is indicated. The Purbeck marble finishing slabs and the flagstone fragments are either from wall decoration or part of an *opus sectile* flooring (for a discussion of Purbeck marble inlay, see Cunliffe 1971, 30).

In Phase XII, *c* AD 250/270–410/420, limestone blocks found in pits 100 and 105 with daub and ash suggest that a building of 4th century date may have been demolished or destroyed by fire, and the pits filled with debris from that structure.

Fragments found in connection with the building of Phase XV, dated to the 8th–11th centuries, were of limestone, with blocks of flint, some with the mortar still attached. It may be that these blocks were used as part of the architrave of a doorway.

Roman window glass: see the glass report.

Tesserae

Mosaic tesserae of chalk, Liassic stone, sedimentary rock, Purbeck marble, tile and pottery, were recovered from the site.

Phase	Chalk	Lias	Sedimentary rock	Purbeck	Tile	Pot
VII	1					
VII/VIII	7	2				
VIII	2					
IX	4					
IXA	3	1				1
X				1		
XI	20	1			1	
XII	2	2				
Post-Roman	3	2	4			

TABLE 5. Materials used for tesserae, by phase

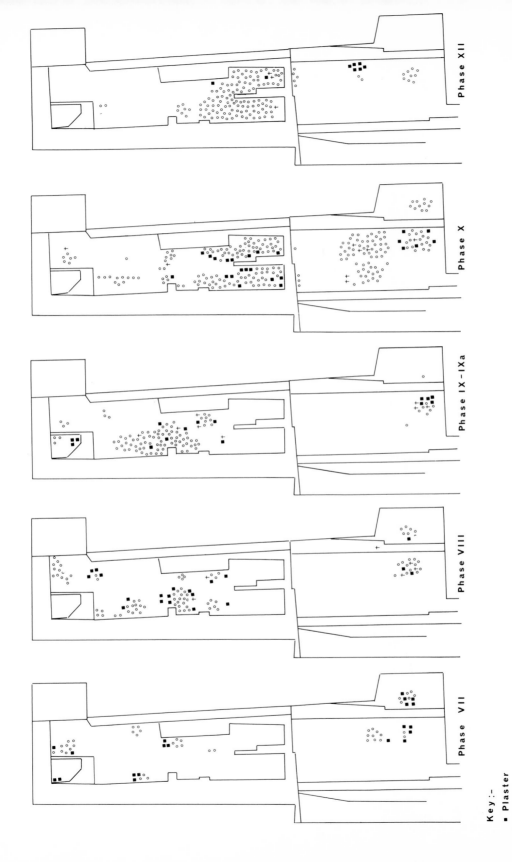

Key:-
■ Plaster
† Tesserae
°° Nails

Phase VII

Phase VIII

Phase IX – IXa

Phase X

Phase XII

Fig 56. Distribution of Roman plaster, tesserae and nails on the site by phases

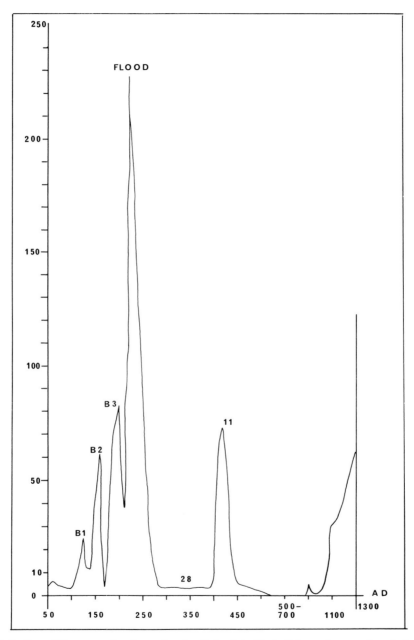

Fig 57. Distribution of Roman and early medieval nails by date (B=building, other numbers indicate levels)

Roman tile and brick

A large quantity of tile and brick was recovered from the excavations, principally from Phases VIII–XII, but also from residual contexts.

Phase	Tiles	Brick	Flue tile	Plaster	Daub	Building stone	Tesserae	Window glass	*Opus signinum*
III									
IV									
V									
VI	×							×	
VII			×	×			×	×	
VII/VIII	×	×	×	×		×	×	×	×
IX	×	×	×	×	×	×	×	×	
IXA	×	×	×	×	×		×	×	
X	×			×		×	×	×	
XI	×	×	×	×		×	×	×	
XII	×	×	×	×	×	×	×	×	

TABLE 6. The distribution of building material by phase in the Roman period

Nails

The nail graph (fig 57) illustrates the number of iron nails retrieved over time. A series of peaks occur, which tie in with major changes in the history of the site.

The slags

JUSTINE BAYLEY (Ancient Monuments Laboratory)

This report was completed by 1979.

The activity indicated by the slags is small-scale iron working. There is smithing slag, much of it in the form of plano-convex hearth bottoms (the pool of slag that collected in the bottom of the hearth), and a number of pieces show traces of the charcoal fuel used. There are also a number of pieces of hearth lining, *ie* clay that has become vitrified on one side from contact with the fire, and a few pieces of completely vitrified clay. The hearth lining and other vitrified clay does not have to be produced by metalworking but, in association with the smithing slag, this is the most likely cause of its formation.

Phase	Context no	Hearth bottom approx diam	Smithing slag	Hearth lining/ vitrified clay
VII	66			Present
VIII	36			Present
	45			Present
	149		Present	Attached to slag
IX	30			Present
X	29	10cm		
XI	143	Part		
XII	11			Present
	77			Present
	100			Present
	28	13×9cm		
XIII	71	9cm	Present	
	121	9×8cm		
XIV	116		Present	
	120			Present
XVI	1			Present
	3		Present	
	8	11×7cm		
XVIII	122		Present	

TABLE 7. Type of slag present, by phase

Animal and human bone

JOHN CHAPMAN, assisted by S WOLFE and W WOODADGE

This report was completed by 1979 and therefore does not take account of subsequent research.

Introduction

The bones recovered from the site were generally in a good condition. All the bones were weighed and counted. Apart from butchery marks, the ribs, vertebrae and loose teeth were excluded from any further analysis. All measurements taken were those defined by von den Driesch (1972) and the horn core classification follows Armitage & Clutton-Brock (1976). No attempt was made at sex determination. The ages are those defined by Silver (1969) for both fusion of limb and tooth eruption. No separation between sheep and goat was made and the term 'sheep' refers to sheep and/or goat. Sieving was not carried out on the site, so the report is biased in favour of the larger animals. The material is stored at Staines with the archival report.

When viewed within each phase, the bone material reflects the developments, recessions and changes in use of the site. The quantities of bone from Phases III–VIA were quite small and have been combined for the purposes of this report. It can be seen from the table of animal bones retrieved (Table 8) that there was a peak in Phase VIII, a decline during Phase IX and a secondary peak during Phase XII. Taken with other evidence, this suggests a small market garden and/or smallholdings. The gradual increase in numbers of bones present during Phases XIII, XIV and XV, reaching a peak during phase XVI, may reflect the growth of the town. After Phase XVI the fall in bone numbers corresponds with a general decline of the town in the late medieval period.

Table 8 shows all the animal bones from each phase; a brief discussion by phase of the more important is on microfiche 44–52. Tables giving the measurements of cattle long bones (Table 9), horse long bones (Table 10) and sheep long bones (Table 11), and of two complete horse skulls (Table 12) are on microfiche 53–56. The Later Bronze Age cow, the dog, fish, bird and human bones are discussed separately below.

Butchery evidence from the site
fig 58

It was difficult to tell with any degree of certainty if the large numbers of broken bones and associated fragments were caused by butchery, accident or the pressure of the overburden – this especially being the case with skulls, pelves and scapulae. Butchery marks were only recorded if they were positively identified. Although cattle showed the highest number of butchered bones, the relatively smaller number of butchery marks on carcasses of pig and sheep could suggest that the meat from these two smaller animals was being distributed on the bone, such as shoulder joints, which would have resulted in these bones being removed from the site.

Butchery techniques employed seemed rather crude compared to modern day methods, and it is likely that the Roman and medieval butchers were only concerned with reducing the carcass into manageable portions and removing as much meat as possible from the bones. The diagram (fig 58) shows the method of disjointing, the shaded areas indicating the percentage of butchery for that area. As the medieval material showed a similar *modus operandi* to the Roman, both periods have been grouped together.

The evidence indicates that cattle of the Roman period were slaughtered and dressed on the site. The animals were probably brought on to the site live, thus solving the problem of transporting the dead weight of the carcass, and the pond (Phase VII/VIII) could have been used by these animals while they awaited slaughter.

Pit 30 (Phase IX) contained a large number of mandibles, most of which had been chopped between the area of the processus articularis and corocoid (hinge area) and the third molar. This might have been to facilitate the removal of the tongue. Modern butchery techniques can

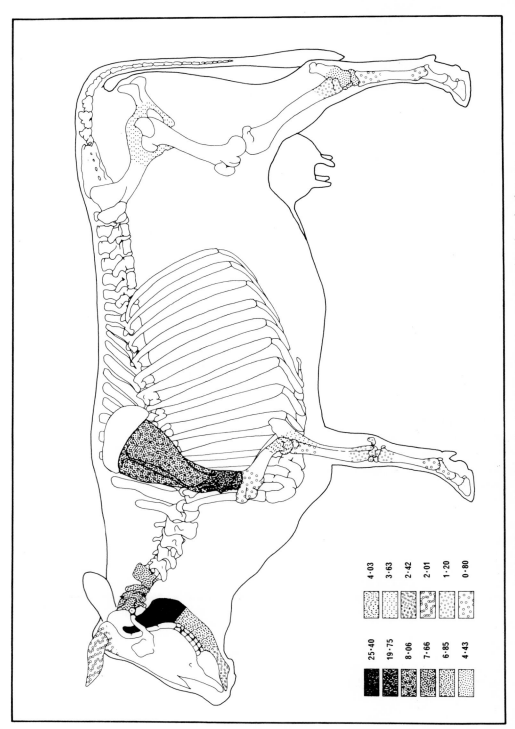

Fig 58. Diagram of butchery cuts; shaded parts indicate percentage of butchery for that area

achieve the same result without going to such extremes and this illustrates how crude the techniques of Roman and medieval butchers were. The large number of hyoids found on the site also indicated tongue removal, whilst marks on the outside of some mandibles could have been the result of the removal of cheek meat.

Compared to the number of skull fragments, such as maxillae, there was an obvious shortage of horn cores. Some of those that were present were porous and were juvenile/sub-adult in age. A pit in the baulk of the 1977 excavation on the Central Area Development (report in preparation) contained a large number of cores which points to their use as raw materials, this possibly being the reason for their absence from the Quakers' site. A small number of skull fragments contained a fragment of horn core, but in most cases an area of the skull was also removed with the core.

Chop marks on the occipital condyles, atlas and epistropheus were probably due to the severing of the head in this region. Horizontal and vertical chop marks were also noted on a number of vertebrae. Although most of the ribs were fragmented, a few of the more complete pieces did show evidence of butchery. The butchery of vertebrae and ribs is not included on fig 58. A consistent method of butchery throughout most periods was the multiple chopping of the scapula fossa, and in some cases a perforation through the blade. This type of butchery is well illustrated by Schmid (1972), where she states that the perforation could be caused by a prong or hook being pushed into the blade while still covered with meat; the joint was then suspended in the chimney to smoke. The forelegs were probably removed beween the distal end of the humerus and the radius and ulna. Four ulnae were chopped extensively on all sides in a distal direction, but the reason for this is unknown.

Two other major areas of butchery were in the pelvis region, due to the removal of the femur from the pelvic girdle, and in the area of the calcanei and astragalus, resulting in the removal of the lower leg which contained little meat, but could have been used for stews or for glue production. There was no evidence for butchery between the femur and the tibia/fibula, but most of the distal articular surfaces of the femur were found separate from the shaft. It is probable, however, that butchery took place in this area.

The evidence for butchery shown by sheep and pig bones was similar to that exhibited by the cattle bones. Two sheep tibia had holes in their distal ends. Similar evidence has been noted by Mrs G Done from the nearby Barclays Bank site (unpublished report). Her report stated that it appears as if some sort of apparatus was used to suspend the carcasses, for example to facilitate stripping of the skin, or immersion in brine or other pickle, though a meat hook under the Achilles tendon would seem to be the simplest and most obvious method. During the post-medieval period a number of pelvic fragments and tibiae had been sawn through in a number of places, but it was not clear if this was caused by butchery or bone working.

There was a preponderance of immature sheep and pig bones which pointed to a preference for lamb and sucking-pig, but there was little bone evidence for veal in the diet.

Evidence for disease and injury

Arthritis

From the bones recovered the most common visible disease recorded was arthropathy.

Five phalanges showed evidence of arthritis. One, from context 28 (Phase XII) had extensive exostosis. The others were rather eburnated on the articular surfaces, indicating that the cartilage of the joint had been destroyed allowing the bones to rub together. A proximal right metatarsal from the horse had lesions over half the surface, most of the articular surface being destroyed. The proximal fragment of an ox metatarsal had some of the tarsals fused to it (tarsitis) which had partly been removed by chopping.

Two pelvic fragments from contexts 10 and 14 both have an acetabulum (articular cavity) with deep eburnation and bony lipping to the articular surface, possibly caused by the dislocation of the femur.

A very large cattle scapula from Phase XVI had large bony lesions, eburnation and lipping of the bone; the arthritis might have been in conjunction with a dislocated humerus, and the joint would probably have been immobilised. Only one dog showed signs of arthritis: a femur had bony lipping across the distal articular surface.

Periodontal disease

Only one sheep mandible showed any evidence of this disease. In this example the disease resulted in the ante-mortem loss of the second premolar and a loosening of a number of other teeth in their sockets caused by the reduction in the bone just below the tooth row.

Healed fractures

A small number of broken ribs were noted, mostly in cattle.

General conclusions

The animal bone material recovered would seemingly reflect the economy of the site. Graphs both of total numbers of fragments and minimum numbers of animals, by species, show curves corresponding to the interpretation of the other evidence from the excavation which was used to assess the importance of each phase. No conclusions could be drawn from the bone material of the early Roman phases due to the small quantity recovered, although it was noted that a high percentage of sheep and pig bones were from immature animals. Apart from those phases and the post-medieval period, the graphs show the same sequence of animals within phases.

The largest number of bones recovered during the excavation were from cattle (57.67%), followed by sheep (21.80%) and pig (11.08%). There was only a small difference in the number of bones from horse (5.33%) and dog (4.12%). Sheep was the only species to be represented in every phase where bone was recorded. Large numbers of cattle, and to a lesser extent sheep, bones are to be expected on a complex urban site, due to their importance in the economy. The cattle could be used for traction and raw materials, as well as the more obvious use for meat, and the sheep used for both wool and meat. Although most of the pigs would have been kept outside the town, a small number might have foraged on household rubbish within the settlement. A number of uses can be suggested for the bone remains recovered during the excavation. The method of butchery, both in the Roman and medieval periods, leads to the conclusion that the site was an area used for the reduction of animal carcasses into manageable sized 'joints'. It is not clear whether the bone represents animals being brought on to the site dead or alive, but the pond rather suggests the latter during the early Roman phases. The small number of horn cores present, compared with other skull fragments, and the evidence for their deliberate removal, may point to their use as raw material elsewhere within the town. A number of knife marks on skull fragments, however, could be interpreted as being caused during the removal of the hide, although no archaeological evidence for horn working or tanning has yet been found within the town. This would also apply to the production of lard and glue.

The use of horse in the diet cannot be ruled out, although the chop marks could be the result of bone working and not necessarily caused by butchery. The Romans thought highly of horses and it was sometimes their practice to bury them outside the settlement area (Grant 1975, 383), which is possibly why so few bones were present in Roman phases. There is, however, an increase in their numbers in Phase XII, which may correspond with the change in the town's character in the later Roman period. During the medieval period Staines was famous for its horse fairs (VCH 1962, 20–1), and this increase in the presence of horses is reflected by a higher percentage of horse bone towards the end of the medieval period. However, as the trade at the horse fairs was in live animals, and not in meat, as with other animals, one would not expect to find the same quantity of bone as for cattle, sheep and pig.

Although a number of bone pins and other bone artefacts were recovered, there was only a small amount of material that could be associated with bone working. No partly worked bone or large amounts of waste material was recovered to suggest bone working in the immediate vicinity.

The immature bones from cattle, sheep and pig can be interpreted either as coming from veal, lamb and sucking-pig, or premature death due to poor veterinary knowledge and a low protein diet.

The prehistoric cow
fig 59; pl 2

A near-complete skeleton of an adult cow (*Bos* sp) was found in a roughly oval pit which cut the flood deposit (61) below the Roman levels. Only a slight depression was noted, the remainder of the pit having been eroded by Roman and modern features. A radiocarbon date (Harwell 1980) from the ribs gives a date of 2820±100 bp (870 bc), *ie* within the Later Bronze Age. The animal was lying on its left side with the head turned back laterally and resting on the thorax. The fore-legs were in a slightly drawn-up position. The right radius, ulna, and left metacarpus were all damaged by a mechanical excavator during the removal of an overlying Quaker grave. This resulted in the loss of all bones from the mid-shaft of the right radius and ulna, together with those from the distal end of the left metacarpus, in a distal direction. A second grave, in the pelvic region, caused damage to the pelvis and resulted in the loss of the coccygeal vertebra.

The right acetabulum was reconstructed for sex identification. The specimen proved to be female (identification by Dr P Armitage). No measurements of the skull were possible as this was also in a fragmented condition, but all the epiphyses were fused and most of the remaining long bones were complete, which allowed R T Jones to take the measurements tabulated on Table 13, microfiche 57. The only sign of any injury was a healed fracture of a rib. No other signs of injury or disease were noted, so the cause of death is unknown. It is probable that the legs were drawn up to accommodate the animal in its pit; this could also be the reason for the position of the head, although it has been suggested that the turning back of the head could be caused by the cow being exposed to the sun's heat on the one side, over a period of days, causing the tendons on that side to contract, thus forcing the head to that side. However, it is not clear why it should have been placed in a pit and then left exposed.

Two other excavations have revealed the skeletons of cows of prehistoric date. At Gussage All Saints (Harcourt 1975) the cow skeleton also contained the bones of a foetus in the process of being born, which enabled the veterinarian to suggest that both had died during the process. The epiphyses of the cow were not fused, therefore no measurements were taken. The animal was about 18 months old at death (BM(NH) Reg No ARC 1973.5669).

Excavations at a Roman fort at Hayton (Johnson 1978, 103) revealed the skeleton of a cow of probable Iron Age date within a pit, this being on the outer lip of the fort ditch. The pit was roughly oval in shape. The cow was on its left side, the legs being drawn up under it and the skull turned back over its fore-legs. The nasal end of the skull was seriously damaged, which may have occurred in Roman times, together with the loss of some of the smaller extremities which were on the lip of the ditch. The withers height can be calculated, using the metacarpal and metatarsal to give 105.6 and 108.6cm respectively (using Fock's factors for cows in von den Driesch & Boessneck 1974). The animal was probably five to six years old.

The evidence for dog

The dog was the fifth most frequently occurring species recovered from the site. In some of the smaller groups there were more dog than horse bones, although on average the figures for dog are slightly below those of horse (see Table 8). Only one bone from Phase III (early Roman) was present. The numbers were higher from the pond and Phase VIII, where there was a first peak, then declined in Phase IX. They rose dramatically for the flood level, Phase XI, and there was no further large increase until Phase XVI. The high percentage of bones recorded for Phase XI is probably due to the redeposition of material from Phases VII to X, caused by the initial flood surge, and that for Phase XVI is probably the result of market gardening and the spreading of rubbish deposits over two centuries; thus the readings for the numbers of dog present may give a false impression. The material from Phases VII/VIII (pond), VIII and IX came from reasonably undisturbed layers, though it must be remembered that the southern edge of all these phases was affected by the flooding of the site in Phase XI and that any conclusions to be drawn must take into account the effect of that flooding.

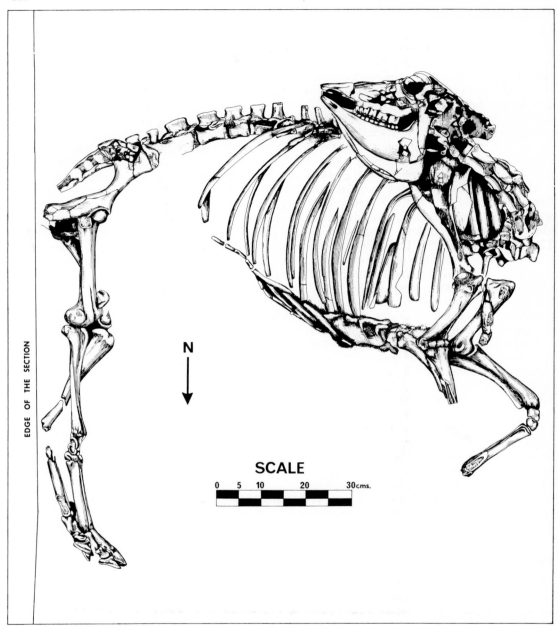

Fig 59. Prehistoric cow skeleton

    Measurements (tabulated in Tables 14 and 15, microfiche 58) were taken of the complete long
bones and skulls and all measurements used are those devised by Harcourt (1974). The skulls
were compared with those from the Harcourt dog collection housed at the Ancient Monuments
Laboratory. Three skulls compared favourably with a Jack Russell (ref 66.21), a beagle (ref
67.4) and a Border collie (ref 64.30). Although these give the archaeologist a general idea as to
the size of the animal, they should not be taken as an indication of breed or appearance.
Measurements of the long bones suggested a division into two sizes of animal. A smaller dog was

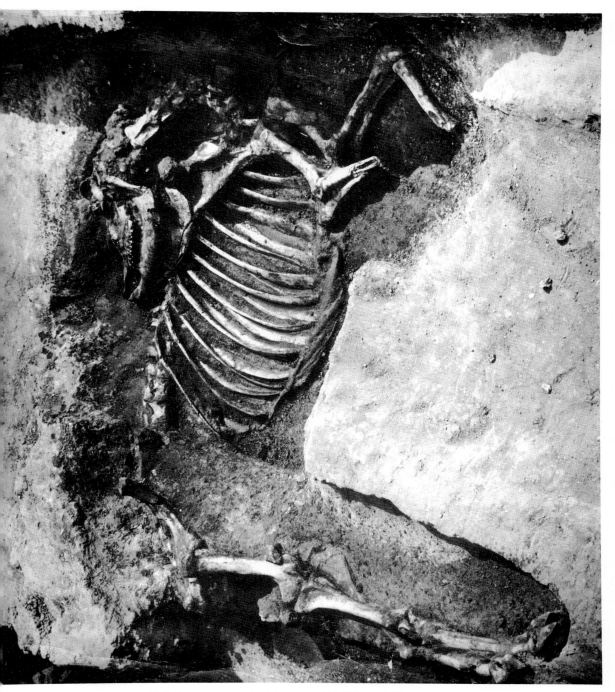

Pl 2. Prehistoric cow burial (approx 1/6) (Photo: J Chapman)

also present, but as the bones were bowed, no measurements were taken. The smaller dogs may have been 'lap dogs' or small hunting dogs, while the larger specimens could have been either guard dogs, hunting dogs or just scavengers around the settlement. The latter can be suggested as the area may have been used as a kill/butchery area, and some gnawed bones were recorded, but it is impossible to tell the use of the dogs from the bone evidence. The Romans were known to have had a high regard for British dogs, references being made to their export during the Iron Age, and later they are depicted on stone reliefs, hunting cup scenes and bronze models, which show the variability of breeds noted by Harcourt.

There is no evidence to show that the dog was used as an additional source of food.

Fish

Few fish remains were recorded (see Table 8), but sieving was not undertaken, and given the fragile nature of fish bones, they could easily have been missed in this rescue excavation. With riparian occupation one would expect fish to play an important part in the general diet.

Most of the bones recovered were fin rays which could not be identified as to species; however, a vertebral centrum from eel (*Anguilla anguilla*) was recorded from contexts 98 (Phase XII) and 156 (Phase XVI). A dentary from chubb/dace (*Cyprinidae*) was present in 97 (Phase XII). Cod (*Gadus morhua*) was present in 7 (Phase XVIII).

The bird bones

A total of 323 bird bones were recovered from the site, of which 296 were identified. These are set out in Table 16 (microfiche 59–60), which shows the frequency of bones, divided into phase and species per phase. The table shows the large numbers of domestic fowl (*Gallus* sp 50.34%) and duck (*Anas* sp 30.13%) which were present in all important phases. Most of these bones are from the wing area and legs of the bird, which could suggest the dividing of the bird away from the site, similar to today's chicken quarters. However, it is likely that the smaller or more perishable bones were not recovered during the excavation, whilst the tarsometatarsus and metacarpus probably reflect the higher survival due to their being two of the strongest bones in the bird skeleton. A radius identified as duck was most similar to a Muscovy duck; this bone comes from context 7 (Phase XVIII).

Goose (*Anser* sp), woodcock (*Scolopax rusticola*), and teal (*Anas crecca*) could be considered as a possible supplement to the Roman diet, and perhaps also dove (*Streptopelia* sp), coot (*Fulica atra*) and starling (*Sturnus vulgaris*), which are still eaten in some countries today. Raven (*Corvus corax*) was the third most commonly occurring species (6.16%), and other scavengers – jackdaw (*Corvus monedula*), rook (*Corvus frugilegus*), buzzard (*Buteo buteo*), and crow (*Corvus corone*) – form the remainder of the bird bones. Most of these birds are, however, only represented by an assortment of single bones. There is, in fact, no reason why they could not have been used as a source of food. Brothwell (1963) has suggested that ravens may have been kept as pets but are more likely, in his opinion, to have been killed for menacing domestic poultry chicks and were probably often present around settlements. This could also apply to the other scavengers found at this site. He also suggests that jackdaws and rooks were exploiters of agricultural land, particularly grasslands, but also of fields sown with cereals, beans, *etc*. Only four bones have been recorded as being immature; these are difficult to identify whilst still porous and relatively featureless (one tarsometatarsus, one femur and two ulnae).

Human bone

The human infant bones from the site were the first to be recovered from an archaeological excavation within the town. They were generally in good condition, although some from deposits 8 and 10 were slightly eroded. Excluding rib fragments, some 70 bones were identified.

The maximum length of the infant bones were measured and compared with measurements of skeletons of known age who lived prior to the Industrial Revolution (R Powers, unpublished). All the bones were relatively the same size and approximately neonatal. The three mandibles were all unfused left sides. One, from context 174, has a deciduous incisor, which is twisted within its cavity and lies below the head of the bone. The second mandible, from 8, is more advanced and has two deciduous teeth, an incisor and a molar. These two teeth are just erupting, which indicates an approximate age of six to seven months old.

In Phase X (174) the bones probably represent the same individual, except for the distal end of a femur which is certainly from another individual. Rib fragments, from 8 and 10, were also present but have not been included in the bone frequency table, Table 17 (microfiche 61).

It was permissible under Roman law to bury infants of under 40 days old inside the town limits. This is probably why all the infant bones from the Roman period were of birth size.

The bones from the site give no indication as to the cause of death, but as infant mortality was high until quite recently, natural causes are likely in most cases. Skeletons are often found in slave quarters or in the settlements of poorer people (Liversidge 1976, 75), where exposure may have been a way of limiting the size of their families.

Only two mature human bones were recovered from the site (contexts 8 and 10), these being a humerus, which has both proximal and distal epiphyses missing, and a second phalanx.

IV   CONCLUSIONS

Phase I

The variety of finished flint implements of Mesolithic date recovered from the site suggests a semi-permanent, perhaps seasonal, settlement, rather than just a flint-working floor. The site, on a gravel spit on the banks of the Thames and its tributaries, would have been ideal for settlement, close to a good water supply and source of fish and wildfowl.

In this advantageous position the establishment of a more permanent camp at the beginning of the Neolithic period seems probable; although there is an absence of early Neolithic material from the site, it is well attested in the Staines area (including a causewayed camp: Robertson-Mackay 1962, 131; and finds from the river: *Berkshire Archael J* **56** (1958) 54–6). The late Neolithic flints and pottery come probably from a settlement in the immediate vicinity, with which it is probable that feature 244 was associated. Although no finds were recovered from this feature its size and shape (fig 3) correspond to other pits of Neolithic date excavated on lowland sites in Britain (*eg* Field *et al* 1964, 352, figs 1, 2), which have been interpreted as corn storage pits.

Occupation in the Early Bronze Age is indicated by the sherds of collared urns and flint implements typical of this period. Although collared urns are normally associated with burials, it is possible that the Staines sherds come from a settlement site. In the late Neolithic and early Bronze Age it would seem that favourable climatic conditions (*cf* Evans 1975, 142) facilitated the silting up and draining of the channels separating the gravel islands, so forming a reasonably large expanse of land suitable for occupation. This could have been utilised by Middle and Later Bronze Age peoples, and it is therefore suggested that features 241–3, 245–8, 264–5, 270–4, probably belong to these periods, although no material was found *in situ*. However, by the Later Bronze Age the gradual climatic deterioration culminated in the flooding of Island 2. A clay deposit sealed the features, the island and the channel fills.

Phase II

This period is characterised by the deposition of orange water-laid clays (285) which form a horizon for this site and effectively divide the prehistoric levels from the Roman. This flooding cannot be later than the Later Bronze Age as the cow burial has a radiocarbon date of 870 ± 100 bc, and cuts into the clay deposit. The absence of any levels datable to the Iron Age presumably indicates either long-term flooding by fast flowing water, hindering the deposition of silts, or that the land was above water, but with little or no vegetational cover so that erosion of the top soil occurred. Whatever the cause, no early or mid-Iron Age material has yet been found from the town. In fact, Iron Age occupation in this area of the Thames Valley Flood Plain is scarce, although occupation of the terraces of the Thames is generally dense (Canham 1976). Belgic pottery groups from the Johnson & Clark site, 1979 (report in preparation), possibly provide evidence of occupation for the end of the Iron Age.

Phases III–VIA

The Roman period clearly begins in Phase III with the digging of ditches 226 and 106 with their square-cut basal channels, and ditch 249, with a cambered gravel surface between (13). To the north of these features was a series of pits, one with a drain running from it. These pits may represent a small wooden structure or a grouping of rubbish and latrine pits. Fragments of Roman pottery were retrieved from within all these features, but none was closely datable.

After a period of time the earlier ditches 226 and 106 had either silted up or been deliberately filled, and two new ditches 102 and 49 were dug along a similar alignment (Phase IV). The possible structure of Phase III had now gone and part of the remaining pits were overlain by a gravel surface (62), edged on the southern side by an interrupted ditch system (63). The gravelled surface was later relaid and extended northward (65) (Phase V). The ditches of Phase IV may have been deliberately filled with gravel and two new ditches dug (234 and 258), these being sub-divided longitudinally, probably by some form of wooden revetment packed with gravel (220).

Later (Phase VI) two large dumps of clay and/or turf (43 and 108) were deposited over the above-mentioned features, so forming two banks, with a deposit of sand in front of the northern bank (176). In Phase VIA the two banks may have been levelled and two ditches (55 and 262) were dug through the remains of the northern bank. To the south a pit (134) was dug, into which eight pottery vessels had been placed; infant bones from the surrounding area are probably to be associated with this group of pottery, which may therefore form a burial group. Cut through the southern bank were ditches 260 and 261. Small quantities of tile and window glass suggest a substantial building somewhere in the town, although not close to this particular area.

All these features show that there was intensive activity over a short period. To interpret any of these ditches as solely for drainage would seem untenable, as they are cut into a naturally well-drained soil. They may be associated with the building of the bridge, and a suggested military post established at this important river crossing.

Phase VII

The settlement grew rapidly during the later 1st century and developed into a small town. Occupation was concentrated along the London–Silchester road and stretched back some 30m from the road frontage. The first building on the Friends' Burial Ground site, of which only the back wall could be excavated, showed a construction technique of external wall timbers set into trenches, the corner posts being set deeper (for similar construction of a late 1st century building at Chelmsford, see Drury 1975, 165). From the material remaining after the building was demolished, it would appear that it had daub and plaster walls, with glass in the windows, and even a hypocaust system and tessellated floor, but only a thatched or possibly wooden shingle roof, as no significant amount of roofing tile was recovered from the pits and layers of this phase. The pit (66) dug against the back wall contained bronze fragments and iron slag mixed with ash and soil, which may indicate that smithing of some sort was associated with the building.

The group of pits to the south of the building may have been for water storage, their green sandy fill seemingly more indicative of a water-laid deposit than simply erosion material from their sides. Possibly these pits were used in conjunction with the smithing activities in this area.

The boundary of the property was marked by the terminal ends of two ditches (231 and 238). These were dug parallel to the gravel surface (13) and to the building. Their basal fill was very similar to that of the pits and may indicate that water lay in the bottoms of the ditches as well. The exit between the two ditches allowed access to a large pond (14) dug during this period. From the large number of pock-marks around the edge of the pond, it would seem that livestock was taken down to water there, the high incidence of dung beetle remains (identified by Dr M Girling, Ancient Monuments Laboratory) adding weight to this theory. The large number of hipposandals may also indicate the presence of livestock. The top fills of the pits and ditches are similar and include a large amount of pottery, bone and small objects. The samian evidence suggests a terminal date c AD 130, and at this time the building was demolished, the nail graph (fig 57) showing a peak at this date also.

The pottery from this phase shows that during the later 1st century the local Staines kilns supplied the bulk of the demand. After c AD 100 there was a gradual influx of larger groups of imported wares: BB1 appeared at this time, as did a greater proportion of Verulamium region wares. The kilns within Staines itself are most likely to have been out of production by c AD 100–120, and the Colne Valley kilns, such as Fulmer and Hedgerley, replaced them. The most important local kiln products were fine wares, mica-dusted and lead-glazed pottery, commencing *c* AD 70, and lasting, for the lead-glazed wares, to *c* AD 120/30, while mica-dusted forms continued in production until *c* AD 180.

Phase VIII

After the demolition of the building recorded in Phase VII a larger building of probable 'box frame' construction was erected, with a gravel courtyard to the east. Only one room lay within the area of excavation, this having a clay floor (270), and the main part of the building lay between the excavation and the known Roman road c 30m to the north.

The building was probably in the style of a typical town house, the main construction being of timber and daub, with *opus signinum* floors and at least one room with a tessellated pavement. Tile evidence suggests that there was a hypocaust system. The walls were rendered with plaster and painted with simple motifs, and this with the presence of window glass indicates a house of some importance. The roof was probably tiled and the presence of brick may indicate that there were some architectural features requiring the use of this material. Outside and to the south of the building were a series of pits and gullies. Presumably 142 and 149 mark the boundary of the land belonging to the house.

The general improvement in the buildings of Roman Staines *c* AD 130 is seen on most excavated sites in the town (*eg* Central Area Development, Barclays Bank, National Westminster Bank), and surely indicates a period of stable economic conditions with increased prosperity, facilitating the re-development of the town. Similar contemporary improvements have been noted at London (Merrifield 1965, 91–3), Verulamium (Frere 1972, 11–112) and other south-east towns and settlements. This increased prosperity is also reflected by the presence of imported wares and goods not only from other parts of Britain, but also from the Continent.

The pond (14), outside the presumed boundary of the building, was probably no longer in use for the watering of livestock, but was gradually being filled with domestic refuse. By the mid-2nd century AD, there are indications of a gradual change in the town's fortunes. It seems that the building was either demolished or partly altered and the rest of the site levelled, and this clearing may be a reflection in the change of use to which the area was put, by the same owners, or may indicate new owners of the land.

Phase IX

During this phase the building of Phase VIII was probably replaced by a smaller building, but of more substantial construction, incorporating stonework. The presence of hypocaust tiles suggests that some of the stonework was used in the foundations of the building, as part of the hypocaust system. The building had such architectural features as plastered walls, tessellated pavements and a tiled roof. South of the building lay a small complex of interconnecting ditches and pits. The large quantities of bone recovered from these features may indicate that this was part of an industrial area dealing with animal products. The evidence from the bones suggests that either complete carcasses or live animals were brought in and butchered on site. The pottery suggests a date *c* AD 150/60–180/90 for this phase.

Phase IXA

By *c* AD 180/90, the Phase IX building had been deliberately dismantled and the whole area cleared (*cf* nail graph, fig 57). This action has been noted at the same date on all other excavated sites in the town. Declines or breaks in occupation of settlements have been recorded at approximately similar dates at Brentford, Southwark, Chelmsford and London (Sheldon & Schaaf 1978, 67); the reason is as yet unclear, but a combination of factors cannot be ruled out, one of them perhaps being political unrest. At Staines, however, in seeming contrast to other south-eastern settlements, there was reoccupation of the town almost immediately, although on a less organised plan.

Phase X

A small timbered building was constructed on an alignment contrary to the road and all previous building lines. This small building was associated with a ditch system. To the north was a series of pits and stake holes enclosing an area of land, presumably the remains of a fence line. The distance of over 5m between stake holes 57 and 147 can be explained by the intervening area being removed by the digging of 19th century graves. Also worthy of mention is the distribution of nails along this line (fig 56). A coin of Caracalla in the base fill of a post pit (59) supports an early 3rd century date for the building and associated features. Late 2nd to early 3rd century colour-coated wares were also present, but samian of the same period is totally absent. This may reflect a disruption in trade caused by the soldiers' and peasants' revolt of *c* AD 180, recorded by Herodian (Thompson 1952, 12) and the trading of samian to Staines apparently did not resume. The building survived until *c* AD 220, when it was probably destroyed by fire, the layers sealing the remains containing burnt material. This may reflect social instability, but could equally have been a simple accident.

Phase XI

The layers sealing the features of Phase X (10 and 143) have been interpreted as a flood deposit, but the absence of much abrasion on the pottery indicates a very short period of movement and quick redeposition, and they may therefore be interpreted as the result of the initial flood surge which cut into underlying levels and redeposited the material as a thick layer of up to 1m in depth. At the south end of the site the deposit (10) had in turn been sealed by a clean silt (9), indicating a period of still water, allowing for a gradual build-up in the silts. The presence of flooding over areas once occupied is one more factor to be taken into account in discussing this period of decline.

The initial flooding (10) must be treated, at present, as a localised phenomenon, as there is little archaeological evidence from other Thames-side sites for a flood at this time. It may have been caused by a combined surge of water from the Thames and Colne rivers, so affecting Staines far more than other sites downstream. The deposition of silt 9, being over a longer term, may be associated with a suspected general rise in sea levels recorded from the Fens and Somerset Levels (Cunliffe 1966, 68–73) which caused a corresponding rise in river levels.

Phase XII

Abandonment following the flooding of Phase XI, and its effects on the site as a whole, cover the period *c* AD 220–250/70. However, the 'black earth' sealing deposits 10 and 143 at the northern end of the site may indicate renewed activity *c* AD 240. The presence of mortaria from Oxfordshire dated *c* AD 240/50 and the coin evidence would seem to confirm this. The area to the south was still affected by water until the 250s or later and the covering of 'black earth' here should probably be dated from the 270s; this is again reflected by coin and pottery evidence.

The 'black earth' seems most likely to have been the result of market gardening. In excavation no differentiation could be seen in the soil from the 3rd century until the 5th century, but features did cut the 'black earth' and were sealed by it, so that a gradual build up in the stratigraphy over the centuries is indicated. The 'black earth' recorded on many Roman sites in south-east England is often sterile of features, but here the ditched enclosure (11) is seen to cut the deposit and later be sealed by it.

To the south of the ditched enclosure (11) were two possible wells (100 and 105), filled with building debris and a heavy concentration of nails (see figs 56–7) which may indicate that the ditched enclosure contained a building. The presence of the two pots in the west ditch could suggest that the building may have been of a religious nature, of late Roman date. In fact, a nearby structure was burnt down and cleared in the last quarter of the 4th century. The top fill of the ditch (11) and the two wells (100 and 105) contained large quantities of burnt daub and tile, worn fragments of typical 4th century pottery, and unabraded sherds of shell-tempered wares.

Phase XIII

This phase sees the introduction of grass-tempered wares, and presumably Saxon occupation. The relationship between the shell-tempered and grass-tempered pottery is unclear, but there are seemingly two distinct pottery traditions here, in the period which bridges the end of the Roman era and the beginning of the Saxon. At the far southern end of the site were the bases of a segmented ditch system with associated post holes. As this system was composed of separate segments it cannot have been meant for drainage. The presence of post holes along the edges and in the ends may indicate some form of fencing. Since much of the top surface had been removed by later activity the full depth of these ditches has not yet been found. A further 90m of this system have been traced around the southern edge of the town, on the Elmsleigh site (Crouch 1976, 87) and on the Central Area Development site (report in preparation), and it may form part of a series of defensive or boundary lines encircling the Saxon settlement. Within the area of the ditch were a number of Saxon features associated with iron-smithing and the grass-tempered pot found in them may indicate a 5th–7th century date (fig 37). The position of this group of features beyond the land utilised by the Romano-British inhabitants may indicate the continued presence of the indigenous population.

Phase XIV

The only positive evidence for the 7th–8th centuries is at present grass-tempered pottery, but this has a long life span and need not reflect continuous occupation throughout the period in question.

The silt deposit filling and sealing features from Phase XIII may be fitted into this time span and might explain the lack of occupational evidence. This silting level was noted on the Elmsleigh and Central Area Development sites (Crouch 1976, 87, in preparation) and a date of 7th–8th centuries seems to be most appropriate.

Late Saxon activity is sparse, represented by only two features, both at the extreme north of the site. Since the site of the mid–late Saxon church is known to be north of the present town (VCH 1962, 27), it is perhaps likely that the main Saxon occupation was centred there.

Phase XV

By the 11th century the village of 'Stana' had become the small thriving market town of 'Stanes' (VCH 1962, 1–33). The expansion of the town is seen by the re-use of land away from the main centre close to the road and church. A building of this period which was partly excavated was probably half-timbered (*cf* nail graph, fig 57) on a clay and pebble foundation and wall, with perhaps a stone doorway. The position of this building so far from the centre of medieval Staines (there is a heavy concentration of medieval material from the Johnson & Clark site 1979, and the Bridgehead sites, 1978 and 1980; fig 1) either suggests that the land close to the centre was becoming scarce for building and therefore expensive, or that the building was deliberately sited close to a water course, as this was needed for some industrial process. The presence of slag in pits 5, 116 and 121 is indicative of smithing and so the building was probably associated with this activity.

The rest of the site was void of features, except for the 'black earth' layer 8, presumably a cultivation soil.

Phase XVI

During the early part of this phase, the continued expansion of the town led to a greater usage of the land to the rear of the High Street. Two separate groups of features belong to this phase. The northern group consisted of a series of pits and post pits and an associated well (38), probably dug at the back of a High Street tenement. The evidence from the slag and small finds suggests a small industrial complex, probably for smithing.

The second group of features, some 30m south, consisted of four pits, all probably wells, which cut the foundations of the building of Phase XV. Material in their backfill suggests a *terminus post quem* late in the 14th century.

The land between the two areas was once again characterised by the ubiquitous 'black earth' (8).

Phase XVII

The lack of later material of 15th–16th century date may be tied to the decline of the town's wealth due to the reduction of the wool trade, to which the fortunes of the town were known to have been strongly linked (Middlesex Records Accession 809/MSS/197, 332, 400). In addition, the heavy disturbance of most of the site by the digging of the graves in the 19th century meant that it was only in the small area outside the graveyard, to the extreme north of the site, that archaeological data could be retrieved. Again the 'black earth' was the only feature, containing material up to the 18th century.

Phase XVIII

The maps of the late 18th–19th century (*eg* OS Middlesex 25″, XIX, *14,* 1865–9) show that the land excavated was the garden of a large house fronting the High Street. The three pits, 6, 7 and 125, were no doubt associated with this building, and dug to take household refuse. Material from the pits was found to be contemporary and coins suggest a date in the 1830s for their filling.

Phase XIX

In 1843 the Society of Friends purchased the garden of the house mentioned under Phase XVIII. On the land was built a Meeting House with a graveyard surrounding it. Beyond the boundary of the graveyard the land was owned by the Ashbys and used for the dumping of the broken and disused bottles from their nearby bottling plant, which were placed in a large pit (250). The Meeting House was pulled down in the 1930s, and the only part of the building surviving to be recognised archaeologically, were the concrete foundations and a well which had been built into the east wall.

BIBLIOGRAPHY

Anderson, A C, 1978 *Roman roughcast beakers,* unpub BA dissertation, Univ Leicester

—, 1980 *Guide to Roman fine wares*

Anderson, A S, & Wacher, J S, 1980 Excavations at Wanborough, Wiltshire, *Britannia,* **11,** 115–26

Apted, M R, Gilyard-Beer, R, & Saunders, A D (eds), 1977 *Ancient monuments and their interpretation*

Armitage, P L, & Clutton-Brock, J, 1976 A system for classification and description of the horn cores of cattle from archaeological sites, *J Archaeol Sci,* **3,** 329–48

Arthur, P, 1978 The lead glazed wares of Roman Britain, in Arthur & Marsh 1978, 293–356

—, & Marsh, G (eds), 1978 *Early fine wares in Roman Britain,* Brit Archaeol Rep, **57**

Babelon, E, 1897 *Catalogue des camées antiques et modernes de la Bibliothèque Nationale*

Barker, D, 1976a Clay pipes, in Crouch 1976, 129–31

—, 1976b Small finds, in Crouch 1976, 121–7

Barrett, J C, 1973 Four Bronze Age cremation cemeteries from Middlesex, *Trans London Middlesex Archaeol Soc,* **24,** 111–34

—, 1976 Deverel–Rimbury: problems of chronology and interpretation, in *Settlement and economy in the third and second millennia BC* (eds C Burgess & R Miket), Brit Archaeol Rep, **33,** 289–307

Biddle, M, 1964 Excavation of a motte and bailey castle at Therfield, Hertfordshire, *J Brit Archaeol Assoc,* **26–7,** 53–91

Bird, J, Graham, A H, Sheldon, H L, & Townend, P (eds), 1978 *Southwark Excavations 1972–4,* London Middlesex Archaeol Soc & Surrey Archaeol Soc Joint Pub, **1**

Blurton, T R, 1977 Excavation at Angel Court, Walbrook, 1974, *Trans London Middlesex Archaeol Soc,* **28,** 14–100

Brailsford, J W, 1962 *Hod Hill, vol 1. Antiquities from Hod Hill in the Durden Collection,* Brit Mus

Brassington, M, 1971 A Trajanic kiln complex near Little Chester, Derby, 1968, *Antiq J*, **51**, 36–69

British Museum 1924 *Guide to mediaeval antiquities*

Brodribb, A C C, Hands, A R, & Walker, D R, 1971a *Excavations at Shakenoak Farm, near Wilcote, Oxfordshire, 1*, 2 edn, privately printed

—, 1971b *Excavations at Shakenoak Farm, near Wilcote, Oxfordshire, 2*, privately printed

—, 1972 *Excavations at Shakenoak Farm, near Wilcote, Oxfordshire 3*, privately printed

—, 1973 *Excavations at Shakenoak Farm, near Wilcote, Oxfordshire, 4*, privately printed

Brothwell, D, 1963 *Digging up bones*, Brit Mus (Natur Hist)

—, & Higgs, E S (eds), 1969 *Science in archaeology*, 2 edn

Brown, A E, & Sheldon, H L, 1970 Highgate 1969, *London Archaeol*, **1**, 150–4

Bushe-Fox, J P, 1913 *Excavations on the site of the Roman town at Wroxeter, Shropshire, in 1912*, Rep Res Com Soc Antiq London, **1**

—, 1915 *Excavations at Hengistbury Head, Hampshire, in 1911–12*, Rep Res Com Soc Antiq London, **3**

—, 1932 *Third report on the excavations of the Roman fort at Richborough, Kent*, Rep Res Com Soc Antiq London, **10**

—, 1949 *Fourth report on the excavations of the Roman fort at Richborough, Kent*, Rep Res Com Soc Antiq London, **16**

Butcher, S A, 1967 in D Dudley, Excavations on Nor'Nour in the Isles of Scilly, 1962–6, *Archaeol J*, **124**, 21–3

—, 1977 Enamels from Roman Britain, in Apted *et al* 1977, 41–70

Callender, M H, 1965 *Roman amphorae*

Calvi, M C, 1968 *I vetri romani del Museo di Aquileia*

Camden, W, 1695 (ed E Gibson) *Camden's Britannia*

Canham, R, 1976 The Iron Age in *The archaeology of the London area: current knowledge and problems* (ed J Kent), London Middlesex Archaeol Soc, Special Paper, **1**, 42–9

—, 1978a *2000 years of Brentford*

—, 1978b Excavations at London (Heathrow) Airport, 1969, *Trans London Middlesex Archaeol Soc*, **29**, 1–44

Carson, R A G, Hill, P V, & Kent, J P C, 1965 *Late Roman bronze coinage, pts 1 and 2*

Castle, S A, 1972 A kiln of the potter Doinus, *Archaeol J*, **129** (1973), 69–88

—, 1976 Roman pottery from Brockley Hill, Middlesex, 1966 and 1972–1974, *Trans London Middlesex Archaeol Soc*, **27**, 206–27

—, 1978 Amphorae from Brockley Hill, *Britannia*, **9**, 383–92

Chaplin, R E, 1971 *The study of animal bones from archaeological sites*

Chapman, H, 1976 The querns, in Crouch 1976, 127

Charlesworth, D, 1959 Roman glass in northern Britain, *Archaeol Aeliana*, 4 ser, **37**, 44–6

—, 1966 Roman square bottles, *J Glass Stud*, **8**, 26–40

Clark, A J, 1949 The fourth-century Romano-British pottery kilns at Overwey, Tilford, *Surrey Archaeol Collect*, **51** (1950), 29–56

Clark, J G D, 1955 A microlithic industry from the Cambridgeshire Fenland and other industries of Sauveterrian affinities from Britain, *Proc Prehist Soc*, **21**, 3–20

—, & Fell, C I, 1953 The early Iron Age site at Micklemoor Hill, West Harling, Norfolk, and its pottery, *Proc Prehist Soc*, **19**, 1–40

Collingwood, R G, & Richmond, I A, 1969 *The archaeology of Roman Britain*

Corder, P, 1941 A Roman pottery of the Hadrianic–Antonine period at Verulamium, *Antiq J*, **21**, 271–98

—, 1943 The Roman pottery made at Fulmer, *Rec Buckinghamshire*, **14**, 153–63

Cotton, M A, 1947 Excavations at Silchester 1938–9, *Archaeologia*, **92**, 121–67

—, & Gathercole, P W, 1958 *Excavations at Clausentum, Southampton, 1951–54*

Cox, D H, 1949 *The excavations at Dura Europos, final report IV, pt I, fasc 2: the Greek and Roman pottery*

Coysh, A W, 1970 *Blue and white transfer ware, 1780–1840*

Croft, P, & Woodadge, W E, 1976 Post-medieval pottery, in Crouch 1976, 114–188

Crossley, D W, 1975 *The Bewl Valley ironworks, Kent, c 1300–1730*, Roy Archaeol Inst Monograph

Crouch, K R, 1976 The archaeology of Staines and the excavation at Elmsleigh House, *Trans London Middlesex Archaeol Soc*, **27**, 71–134

Crummy, N, 1979 A chronology of Romano-British bone pins, *Britannia*, **10**, 157–63

Cunliffe, B, 1964 *Winchester excavations 1949–1960, 1*

—, 1966 The Somerset Levels in the Roman period, in Thomas 1966, 68–73

—, 1968 (ed) *Fifth report on the excavations at the Roman fort at Richborough, Kent*, Rep Res Com Soc Antiq London, **23**

—, 1969 *Roman Bath*, Rep Res Com Soc Antiq London, **24**

—, 1970 The Saxon culture sequence at Portchester Castle, *Antiq J*, **50**, 69–71

—, 1971 *Excavations at Fishbourne, 1961–9, vol 2: the finds*, Rep Res Com Soc Antiq London, **27**

—, 1975 *Excavations at Portchester Castle, 1: Roman*, Rep Res Com Soc Antiq London, **32**

—, & Phillipson, D W, 1968 Excavations at Eldons Seat, Encombe, Dorset, *Proc Prehist Soc*, **34**, 191–237

Curle, A O, 1923 *The treasure of Traprain. A Scottish hoard of Roman silver plate*

de Laet, S J, 1950 Een Gallo-Romeins heiligdom op de Steenberg te Hofstade bij Aalst (Oostvlaanderen), *Cultureel Jaarb Provincie Oostvlaanderen*, **1–46**, 269–314

Detsicas, A P (ed), 1973 *Current research in Romano-British Coarse Pottery*, Counc Brit Archaeol Res Rep, **10**

Dore, J, & Greene, K (eds), 1977 *Roman pottery studies in Britain and beyond. Papers presented to John Gillam, July 1977*, Brit Archaeol Rep Supp Ser, **30**

Down, A, 1974 *Chichester Excavations 2*

—, 1978 *Chichester Excavations 3*

— & Rule, M, 1971 *Chichester Excavations 1*

Drury, P J, 1975 Chelmsford, in Rodwell & Rowley 1975, 159–73

Dudley, D, 1967 Excavation on Nor'Nour in the Isles of Scilly, *Archaeol J*, **124**, 1–64 du Plat Taylor, J, & Cleere, H (eds), 1978 *Roman shipping and trade: Britain and the Rhine provinces,* Counc Brit Archaeol Res Rep, **24**

Durham, B, 1976 Archaeological investigations in St Aldates, Oxford, *Oxoniensia,* **42** (1978), 83–203

Evans, J G, 1975 *The environment of early man in the British Isles*

Farley, M, 1976 Saxon and medieval Walton, Aylesbury: excavations 1973–4, *Rec Buckinghamshire,* **20**, pt 2

Farrar, R A H, 1973 The techniques and sources of Romano-British black-burnished ware, in Detsicas 1973, 67–103

Field, N H, Matthews, C L, & Smith I F, 1964 New Neolithic sites in Dorset and Bedfordshire, with a note on the distribution of Neolithic storage pits in Britain, *Proc Prehist Soc,* **30**, 352–81

Fölzer, E, 1913 *Die bilderschüsseln der ostgallischen Sigillata–manufakturen. Römische keramik in Trier, 1*

Fox, A, & Ravenhill, W, 1972 The Roman fort at Nanstallon, Cornwall, *Britannia,* **3**, 56–111

Frere, S S, 1964 Excavations at Dorchester on Thames, 1962, *Archaeol J,* **119**, 114–49

—, 1972 *Verulamium Excavations I,* Rep Res Com Soc Antiq London, **28**

—, 1974 *Britannia,* 2 edn

—, & St Joseph, J K, 1974 The Roman fortress at Longthorpe, *Britannia,* **5**, 1–129

Fulford, M G, 1975a The pottery, in Cunliffe 1975, 270–367

—, 1975b *New Forest Roman pottery,* Brit Archaeol Rep, **17**

Garbsch, J, 1975 Zu neuen römischen funden aus Bayern, *Bayerische Vorgeschichts Blatter,* **40**, 68–73

Gardner, E, 1924 Bronze Age urns of Surrey, *Surrey Archaeol Collect,* **35**, 1–29

Gentry, A, Iven, J, & McClean, H, 1977 Excavations at Lincoln Road, London Borough of Enfield, Nov 1974–March 1976, *Trans London Middlesex Archaeol Soc,* **28**, 101–89

Gillam, J P, 1970 *Types of Roman coarse pottery vessels in northern Britain,* 3 edn

Godden, G A, 1971 *Mason's patent ironstone china*

Gose, E, 1950 *Gefässtypen der römischen keramik im Rheinland,* Bonner Jahrb Beiheft, **1**

Grant, A, 1975 The animal bones, in Cunliffe 1975, 378–408

Gray, H, 1977, *Gray's anatomy,* 15 edn

Greene, K, 1978 Roman trade between Britain and the Rhine provinces: the evidence of pottery to *c* AD 250, in du Plat Taylor & Cleere 1978, 52–8

Grimes, W F, 1930 Holt, Denbighshire: the works depot of the Twentieth Legion at Castle Lyons, *Y Cwmmrodor,* **41**

Guido, M, 1978 *The glass beads of the prehistoric and Roman periods in Britain and Ireland,* Rep Res Com Soc Antiq London, **35**

Hammerson, M J, 1978 The coins, in Bird *et al* 1978, 587–600

—, 1980, *Romano-British copies of the coinage of AD 330–48,* unpub MPhil thesis, Univ London

Hanworth, R, & Tomalin, D J, 1977 *Brooklands, Weybridge: the excavation of an Iron Age and*

medieval site, 1964–5 and 1970–1, Res Vol Surrey Archaeol Soc, **4**

Harcourt, R A, 1974 The dog in prehistoric and early historic Britain, *J Archaeol Sci,* **1**, 151–74

—, 1975 *The animal bones from Gussage-All-Saints, Dorset. Report to the Ancient Monuments Laboratory, 1804*

Harden, D B, 1936 *Roman glass from Karanis*

Hartley, B R, 1960 *Notes on the Roman pottery industry in the Nene Valley,* Peterborough Mus

—, 1960–1 The samian ware, in Steer 1960–1, 100–10

—, 1971 The samian pottery, in Brassington 1971, 44–6

—, 1972 The samian ware, in Frere 1972, 216–62

Hartley, K F, 1972 The mortarium stamps, in Frere 1972, 371–81

—, 1977 Two major potteries producing mortaria in the first century AD, in Dore & Greene 1977, 5–17

Hayes, J W, 1975 *Roman and pre-Roman glass in the Royal Ontario Museum*

Helm, P R, 1975–6 Phoenix rising – an introduction to Hilditch, *Northern Ceram Soc J,* **2**, 39–66

Henig, M, 1969 The gemstones from the main drain, in Cunliffe 1969, 71–88

—, 1970 A new cameo from Lincolnshire, *Antiq J,* **50**, 338–40

—, 1971 The huntsman intaglio from South Shields, *Archaeol Aeliana,* 4 ser, **49**, 215–30

—, 1974 *A corpus of Roman engraved gemstones from British sites, pt I,* Brit Archaeol Rep, **8**

Henkel, F, 1913 *Die römischen fingerringe der Rheinland*

Holmes, J M, 1949 Romano-British cemeteries at Haslemere and Charterhouse, *Surrey Archaeol Collect,* **51**, 3–25

Huggins, P J, & Huggins, R M, 1970 Waltham Abbey monastic site and prehistoric evidence, 1953–67, *Trans Essex Archaeol Soc,* **2**, pt 3, 216–44

—, 1973 Excavation of a monastic forge and Saxo-Norman enclosure, Waltham Abbey, *Trans Essex Archaeol Soc,* **5**, 127–84

—, 1976 The excavation of an 11th century Viking hall and 14th century rooms at Waltham Abbey, Essex, *Medieval Archaeol,* **20**, 75–133

Hull, M R, 1963 *The Roman potters' kilns of Colchester,* Rep Res Com Soc Antiq London, **21**

—, 1967 in Dudley 1967, 28–30

—, 1971 The brooches, in Cunliffe 1971, 100–7

Hunter, A G & Kirk, J R, 1952–3 Excavations at Campsfield, Kidlington, Oxon, 1949, *Oxoniensia,* **17–18** (1954), 36–62

Hurst, H, 1972 Excavations at Gloucester 1968–71, first interim report, *Antiq J,* **52**, 24–69

Hurst, J G, 1961 The kitchen area of Northolt Manor, Middlesex, *Medieval Archaeol,* **5**, 211–99

Isings, C, 1957 *Roman glass from dated finds*

Jenkins, F, 1958 The cult of the 'pseudo-Venus' in Kent, *Archaeol Cantiana,* **72**, 60–76.

Jesson, M, & Hill, D (eds), 1971 *The Iron Age and its hill-forts*

Johnson, B, 1975 *Archaeology and the M25*

Johnson, S, 1978 Excavations at Hayton Roman fort, 1975, *Britannia,* **9**, 57–114

Jones, M U, Evison, V I, & Myres, J N L, 1968 Cropmark sites at Mucking, Essex, *Antiq J,* **48**, 210–30

Jones, P, 1982 Saxon and early medieval Staines, *Trans London Middlesex Archaeol Soc*, **33**, 186–213

—, & Shanks, S A, 1976 Saxon and medieval pottery, in Crouch 1976, 101–14

Jones, R, 1974 *Computer based osteometric archaeozoology. Report to the Ancient Monuments Laboratory, 2333*

Jope, E M, & Pantin, W A, 1958 The Clarendon Hotel, Oxford, *Oxoniensia*, **23**, 1–84

Karnitsch, P, 1959 *Die reliefsigillata von Ovilava*

Kellner, H J, 1971 *Die Römer in Bayern*

Knorr, R, 1919 *Töpfer und fabriken verzierter terra-sigillata des ersten jahrhunderts*

—, 1952 *Terra-sigillata-gefässe des ersten jahrhunderts mit töpfernamen*

Lawrence, H, 1974 *Yorkshire pots and potteries*

Lawson, A S, 1976 Shale and jet objects from Silchester, *Archaeologia*, **105**, 259–75

Liversidge, J, 1976 *Everyday life in the Roman empire*

Lockett, T A, 1972 *Davenport pottery and porcelain, 1794–1887*

London Museum, 1940 *Medieval catalogue*, London Mus Catalogue, **7**

Longley, D, 1976 Excavations on the site of a Late Bronze Age settlement at Runnymede Bridge, Egham, *London Archaeol*, **3**, 10–17

—, & Needham, S, 1979 Egham: A late Bronze Age settlement and waterfront, *Current Archaeol*, **68**, 262–7

Lowther, A W G, 1949 Excavations at Purberry Shot, Ewell, Surrey, *Surrey Archaeol Collect*, **50**, 9–46

Lutz, M, 1970 *L'atelier de Saturninus et de Satto à Mittelbronn (Moselle)*, Gallia Supp, **22**

Lyne, M A B, & Jefferies, R S, 1979 *The Alice Holt/Farnham Roman pottery industry*, Counc Brit Archaeol Res Rep, **30**

Mackreth, D, 1981 The brooches, in Partridge 1981, 130–51

Marsden, P R V, 1965 A boat of the Roman period discovered on the site of New Guy's House, Bermondsey, 1958 *Trans London Middlesex Archaeol Soc*, **21**, pt 2, 118–31

Marsh, G, 1978 Early second century fine wares in the London area, in Arthur & Marsh 1978, 119–224

—, & Tyers, P A 1978 The Roman pottery from Southwark, in Bird *et al* 1978, 533–82

Merrifield, R, 1965 *The Roman city of London*

Miller, S N, 1922 *The Roman fort at Balmuildy*

Myres, J N L, 1969 *Anglo-Saxon pottery and the settlement of England*

Neal, D S, 1974 *The excavation of the Roman villa in Gadebridge Park, Hemel Hempstead*, Rep Res Com Soc Antiq London, **31**

Oakley, K P, Vulliamy, C E, Rouse, E C, & Cottrill, F, 1937 The excavation of a Romano-British pottery kiln site near Hedgerley, *Rec Buckinghamshire*, **13**, 252–80

O'Connell, M, & Needham, S, 1977 A Late Bronze Age hoard and settlement at Petters Sports Field, Egham, Surrey, *London Archaeol*, **3**, 123–30

O'Neil, B H St J, 1958 Old Windsor, *Medieval Archaeol*, **2**, 183–5

Orton, C, 1977 The Roman pottery, in Blurton 1977, 30–53

Oswald, F, 1936–7 *Index of figure-types on terra sigillata (samian ware)*

—, 1948 *The commandant's house at Margidunum, Nottingham*

Partridge, C, 1981 *Skeleton Green. A Late Iron Age and Romano-British site*, Britannia Monograph, **2**

Peacock, D P S, 1971 Roman amphorae in pre-Roman Britain, in Jesson & Hill 1971, 161–88

—, 1974a Roman amphorae: typology, fabric and origins, *Mélanges Ecole Française Rome*, **10**, 258

—, 1974b Amphorae and the Baetican fish industry, *Antiq J*, **54**, 231–43

—, 1977a, Ceramics in Roman and medieval archaeology, in Peacock 1977b, 21–33

— (ed), 1977b *Pottery and early commerce. Characterization and trade in Roman and later ceramics*

—, 1978 The Rhine and the problem of Gaulish wine in Britain, in du Plat Taylor & Cleere 1978, 49–51

Penn, W S, 1957 The Romano-British settlement at Springhead: excavation of the bakery site A, *Archaeol Cantiana*, **71**, 53–102

Piggott, S, 1954 *The Neolithic cultures of the British Isles*

Potter, T, 1977 The Biglands mile fortlet, Cumberland, *Britannia*, **8**, 149–84

Radford, C A R, 1932 Small objects in metal, bone, glass, *etc*, in Bushe-Fox 1932, 76–93

Rae, A, & Rae, V, 1974 The Roman fort at Cramond, Edinburgh: excavations 1954–66, *Britannia*, **5**, 163–224

Rahtz, P, & ApSimon, A M, 1962 Excavations at Shearplace Hill, Sydling St Nicholas, Dorset, England, *Proc Prehist Soc*, **28**, 289–328

Richmond, I, 1968 *Hod Hill Vol 2. Excavations carried out between 1951 and 1958 for the Trustees of the British Museum*, Brit Mus

Rivet, A L, & Smith, C, 1979 *The place-names of Roman Britain*

Robertson, A, Scott, M, & Keppie, L, 1975 *Bar Hill: A Roman fort and its finds*, Brit Archaeol Rep, **16**

Robertson-Mackay, R, 1962 The excavation of the causewayed camp, Staines, Middx, *Archaeol Newsletter*, **7**, 131–4

Rodwell, W, & Rowley, T, 1975 *The small towns of Roman Britain*, Brit Archaeol Rep, **15**

Rogers, G B, 1974 *Poteries sigillées de la Gaule Centrale, 1: les motifs non figurés*, Gallia Supp, **28**

Rouvier-Jeanlin, M, 1975 Les figurines gallo-romaines en terre cuite blanche, *Céramique en Gaule Romaine*, Dossiers Archéol, **9**, 95–103

Sanders, J, 1973 *Late Roman shell-gritted ware in southern Britain*, unpub BA dissertation, Univ London

Saunders, C, & Havercroft, L A B, 1977 A kiln of the potter Oastrius and related excavations at Little Munden Farm, Bricket Wood, *Hertfordshire Archaeol*, **5**, 109–156

Schaetzen, P, & Vanderhoeven, M, 1953–4 La terra sigillata à Tongres, *Bull Inst Archéol Liégeois*, **70** (1955)

Schmid, E, 1972 *Atlas of animal bones*

Sharpe, M, 1913 *The Middlesex district in Roman times, pts 1 & 2*

—, 1932 *Middlesex in British, Roman and Saxon times*

Sheldon, H L, 1975 A decline in the London settlement, AD 150–250? *London Archaeol*, **2**, 278–84

—, & Schaaf, L, 1978 A survey of Roman sites in Greater London, in *Collectanea Londiniensia: studies presented to Ralph Merrifield* (eds J Bird, H Chapman & J Clark), London Middlesex Archaeol Soc Special Paper, **2**, 59–88

Shepherd, J D, 1978 *A preliminary study of the base designs of mould-blown glass bottles,* unpub BA dissertation, Univ London

Sheppard, D, 1975 Two Bronze Age urns from Kempton Park, *Trans London Middlesex Archaeol Soc,* **26**, 281–2

Sieveking, G de G, 1968 *Flint implements,* Brit Mus

Silver, I A, 1969 The ageing of domestic animals, in Brothwell & Higgs 1969, 283–302

Simpson, F G, 1913 Excavations on the line of the Roman Wall in Cumberland during the years 1909–12, *Trans Cumberland Westmorland Antiq Archaeol Soc,* new ser, **13**, 297–397

Simpson, G, & Rogers, G B, 1969 Cinnamus de Lezoux et quelques potiers contemporains, *Gallia,* **27**, 3–14

Sissons, S, & Grossman, J D, 1938 *Anatomy of domestic animals*

Smedley, N, & Owles, E, 1961 Some Suffolk kilns: two kilns making colour-coated ware at Grimstone End, Pakenham, *Suffolk Inst Archaeol,* **28**, 203–25

Spence Bate, G, 1866 On the discovery of a Romano-British cemetery near Plymouth, *Archaeologia,* **40**, 500–9

Stanfield, J A, & Simpson, G, 1958 *Central Gaulish potters*

Steer, K A, 1960–1 Excavations at Mumrills Roman fort 1958–60, *Proc Soc Antiq Scotland,* **94**, 86–132

Stukeley, W, 1726 *Itinerarium curiosum* (reprint 1969)

Sutherland, C H V, 1947 The coins, in C F C Hawkes & M R Hull, *Camulodunum,* Rep Res Com Soc Antiq London, **14**, 142–67

Swanton, M J, 1973 *The spearheads of the Anglo-Saxon settlements,* Roy Archaeol Inst Monograph

Tebbutt, C F, 1934 A cist in the Isles of Scilly, *Antiq J,* **14**, 302–4

Terrisse, J-R, 1968 *Les céramiques sigillées des Martres-de-Veyre (Puy-de-Dôme),* Gallia Supp, **19**

Tester, P J, & Bing, H F, 1949 A first century urn-field at Cheriton, near Folkestone, *Archaeol Cantiana,* **62**, 21–36

Thomas, C (ed), 1966 *Rural settlement in Roman Britain,* Counc Brit Archaeol Res Rep, **7**

Thompson, E A, 1952 Peasant revolt in late Roman Gaul and Spain, *Past & Present,* **2**, 11–23

Towner, D C, 1957 *English cream-coloured earthenware*

Toynbee, J M C 1962 *Art in Roman Britain*

—, 1964 *Art in Britain under the Romans*

VCH 1962 *The Victorian history of the counties of England. A history of Middlesex, 3*

von den Driesch, A 1972 *A guide to the measurement of animal bones from archaeological sites,* Peabody Mus Bull, **1**

—, & Boessneck, J, 1974 Kritische anmerkungen zur widerristhöhenberechnung aus längenmassen vor- und frühgeschichtlicher tierknochen, *Säugetierkundliche Mitteilungen,* **22**, 325–48

Wacher, J, 1975 *The towns of Roman Britain*

Wainwright, G J, 1972 Excavation of a Neolithic settlement on Broome Heath, Ditchingham, Norfolk, *Proc Prehist Soc,* **38**, 1–97

—, & Longworth, I H, 1971 *Durrington Walls excavations 1966–8,* Rep Res Com Soc Antiq London, **29**

Warren, S E, 1977 Excavation of a Neolithic site at Sefton Street, Putney, London, *Trans London Middlesex Archaeol Soc,* **28**, 1–13

Waugh, H, & Goodburn, R, 1972 The non-ferrous objects, in Frere 1972, 115–62

Webster, G, 1978 *Boudica: the British revolt against Rome AD 60*

Wedlake, W J, 1958 *Excavations at Camerton, Somerset,* privately printed

Westall, P, 1930 The Romano-British cemetery at The Grange, Welwyn, Herts, *St Albans Hertfordshire Archit Archaeol Soc Trans,* **1**, 37–55

Wheeler, R E M, 1943 *Maiden Castle, Dorset,* Rep Res Com Soc Antiq London, **12**

—, & Wheeler, T V, 1932 *Report on excavations of the prehistoric, Roman and post Roman site in Lydney Park, Gloucestershire,* Rep Res Com Soc Antiq London, **9**

Whitehead, J & C, 1798 *James and Charles Whitehead catalogue* (reprint 1973)

Whiter, L, 1970 *Spode*

Williams, A, 1947 Canterbury excavations in 1945, *Archaeol Cantiana,* **60**, 68–100

Williams, D F, 1977 The Romano-British black burnished industry, in Peacock 1977b, 163–220

Wilson, M G, 1968 Other objects of bronze, iron, silver, lead, bone and stone, in Cunliffe 1968, 93–110

—, 1972 Catalogue of the pottery, in Frere 1972, 265–365

Wood, M, 1976 The glass, in Crouch 1976, 127–9

Woodfield, C C, 1965 Six turrets on Hadrian's Wall, *Archaeol Aeliana,* 4 ser, **43**, 87–200

Wright, L, 1960 *Clean and decent*

Young, C J, 1977 *The Roman pottery industry in the Oxford region,* Brit Archaeol Rep, **43**

ACKNOWLEDGEMENTS

We would like to thank the members of the Spelthorne Archaeological Field Group and our temporary paid assistants for their help with the excavation, which was carried out by a full-time team of Kevin Crouch, Anne Anderson, Roy Hooper, Philip Jones and Susan Shanks. Financial assistance came from the Department of the Environment and from Spelthorne Borough Council; the latter also provided accommodation for processing the finds.

We are most grateful to the following for their assistance during the preparation of this report: Dr Philip Armitage, Paul Arthur, Morag Barton, Joanna Bird, Hugh Chapman, John Cherry, John Clark, Geraldene Done, Alec Down, Alison Goodall, Ian Goodall, C M Green, Dr D B Harden, F W Holling, Alison Locker, Malcolm Lyne, S A McKenna, Roger Jones, the late H Russell Robinson, Charles Ross, Dr D F Williams, Mary Wood, Dr C J Young, and the staffs of Aylesbury Museum, the British Museum, Reading Museum and Verulamium Museum.

The illustrations for this volume have been prepared by the following—drawings: John Barrett (prehistoric pottery), K R Crouch (map, site plans and sections, Roman pottery), K F Hartley (mortaria stamps), Philip Jones (flints, decorated samian, small finds, Saxon and medieval pottery, and prehistoric cow skeleton) and Susan Shanks (Roman and post-medieval pottery); photographs: Ashmolean Museum, John Chapman and Robert Wilkins.

Editor's note: the reports in this volume were substantially completed by 1979, and therefore do not take account of subsequent research and excavation.